LAUNCH YOUR CAREER

LAUNCH YOUR CAREER

—

How ANY Student Can Create Relationships with Professionals and Land the Jobs and Internships They Want

SEAN O'KEEFE

in partnership with
The Career Leadership Collective

Forewords by
La'Tonya Rease Miles, Nationally Recognized First-Generation Student Expert
Barry Posner, Coauthor of *The Leadership Challenge* and *Leadership Practices Inventory*

BK®

Berrett–Koehler Publishers, Inc.

Berrett-Koehler Publishers, Inc.
1333 Broadway, Suite 1000
Oakland, CA 94612–1921
Tel: (510) 817–2277
Fax: (510) 817–2278
www.bkconnection.com

ORDERING INFORMATION

Quantity sales. Special discounts are available on quantity purchases by corporations, associations, and others. For details, contact the "Special Sales Department" at the Berrett-Koehler address above.

Individual sales. Berrett-Koehler publications are available through most bookstores. They can also be ordered directly from Berrett-Koehler:
Tel: (800) 929–2929; Fax: (802) 864–7626; www.bkconnection.com.

Orders for college textbook / course adoption use. Please contact Berrett-Koehler: Tel: (800) 929–2929; Fax: (802) 864–7626.

Distributed to the U.S. trade and internationally by Penguin Random House Publisher Services.

Berrett-Koehler and the BK logo are registered trademarks of Berrett-Koehler Publishers, Inc.

Printed in Canada

Berrett-Koehler books are printed on long-lasting acid-free paper. When it is available, we choose paper that has been manufactured by environmentally responsible processes. These may include using trees grown in sustainable forests, incorporating recycled paper, minimizing chlorine in bleaching, or recycling the energy produced at the paper mill.

Library of Congress Cataloging-in-Publication Data

Names: O'Keefe, Sean, author. |
   Career Leadership Collective (Fort Collins, Colorado), author.
Title: Launch your career : how any student can create relationships with
   professionals and land the jobs and internships they want / Sean O'Keefe;
in partnership with The Career Leadership Collective.
Description: First Edition. | Oakland : Berrett-Koehler Publishers, 2021. |
   Includes bibliographical references and index.
Identifiers: LCCN 2021005951 | ISBN 9781523092680 (paperback) | ISBN
   9781523092697 (adobe pdf) | ISBN 9781523092703 (epub)
Subjects: LCSH: College students--Employment. | College
   students--Vocational guidance.
Classification: LCC HD6276.5 .O54 2021 | DDC 650.14--dc23
LC record available at https://lccn.loc.gov/2021005951

First Edition
27 26 25 24 23 22 21   10 9 8 7 6 5 4 3 2 1

Book production and design: Seventeenth Street Studios
Cover design: Kim Scott, Bumpy Design

CONTENTS

A MESSAGE FROM THE CAREER LEADERSHIP COLLECTIVE

The Career Leadership Collective is extremely delighted to partner with Sean O'Keefe and the Career Launch movement to bring the equitable solutions inside this book to college career centers, faculty, staff, and hundreds of thousands of college students who need and deserve it.

Our National Alumni Career Mobility surveys show that the most important indicators of significant career mobility for students are designing a career plan, receiving helpful career advice, interacting with employers, and seeking career-relevant internships. Career Launch's programs, including this book, help students in all four of these important areas.

I've spent twenty-plus years in career services, and Career Launch's equitable and multimodality programming is one of a kind. Not only do students directly benefit but also career services professionals, faculty, and student success professionals directly benefit by having resources to be more productive during student interactions and by having high-impact asynchronous resources, which allows them to scale their impact.

This book and Career Launch's offerings are easily integrated into for-credit courses and cocurricular programing alike. I encourage higher education professionals to look into Career Launch's certified coach/faculty programs. We have seen so many students' lives change for the better because of the Career Launch methodologies, and we've seen macro-level improvements to student employment outcomes, retention rates, and social mobility through our partnership programs.

I'm glad you are reading or listening to this book and are now part of the Career Launch movement too!

Jeremy Podany
Founder & CEO, The Career Leadership Collective

Learn more about our partnership at
www.careerleadershipcollective.com/careerlaunch.

FOREWORD

La'Tonya Rease Miles, PhD

Nationally Recognized First-Generation Student Expert

My son was one of the nearly two million graduates in the class of 2020 whose college career ended with a whimper due to COVID-19. He was a business major with internship experience, but his goal of working in sports management was put on pause by the pandemic.

Although my son had it tough, many students have it even tougher. I know this because I've worked directly with students at UCLA and Loyola Marymount University for the past sixteen years, especially with first-generation college students, low-income students, and other students who navigate college with big dreams but little social capital.

Sean O'Keefe understands the needs of today's diverse student body—their feelings, doubts, and eagerness. Sean is like a personal coach and cheerleader, always assuring and affirming, never dismissive or trite. His advice is especially helpful for students who do not have family connections or a broad professional network upon which to draw. The Career Launch Method demonstrates that you can build your own network and, perhaps more significantly, why it matters to have connections to professionals in the first place.

The advice in *Launch Your Career* is accessible, easy to follow, and easy to digest. The book is filled with practical exercises and is easy to incorporate into college courses and cocurricular programs. In fact, one of the book's core strengths is its adaptability.

Whether you are attending a four-year university as an undergrad or graduate student, or a community college, or are a returning adult student seeking a certificate and new skills, *Launch Your Career* will serve you well and should be revisited periodically. Even I, a higher education professional and the parent of a college graduate, learned a lot.

While many students these days are told often about the value of building relationships with professionals and about the need to cultivate their brand, *Launch Your Career* has a unique and timeless message to send: it is important to work smart and not just work hard. In other words, have a strategy and a plan. Some people may be shocked to learn that the "best" candidates do not always get the jobs. *Launch Your Career* delivers a kind of straight talk (full of pep and affirmation) that will minimize your fears, prepare you to step out of your comfort zone, and propel you to start taking action.

FOREWORD

Barry Posner, PhD
Coauthor, *The Leadership Challenge*
and *Leadership Practices Inventory*

If you think you are too small to make a difference, try sleeping in a closed room with a mosquito. The truth is that you matter, and you *will* make your mark upon the world. Keep this in mind as you read this book and prepare to adopt the Career Launch Method.

Ask yourself, what do you truly desire? How serious are you about finding an internship or landing a job you really want? Are you just going through the motions? A key point of this book, as the subtitle states, is that *any* student can land the internships and jobs they want, and that's another truth. The research, strategies, tactics, and lessons in this book are applicable to you—no matter your circumstances, setting, personality, background, grades, or program of study.

I met Sean O'Keefe more than fifteen years ago, when he was a graduate student in a study abroad course I was teaching. We struck up a conversation—at his initiative—on a thirteen-hour flight to Korea. He told me about his background and his experience of overcoming long odds to land competitive internships, and then a very competitive full-time position, after finishing his undergraduate degree. He also shared his gratitude for the people who had helped him along the way. He made it a point to tell me that he felt compelled to "pay it forward" and help current students.

Initially, as he was less than six or seven years out of college, it seemed that he could be, at best, a great alumni guest speaker. As the conversation continued, it occurred to me that Sean might be an effective adjunct professor for a new course in the business school for first-year students on leadership. Upon his graduation with an MBA, I alerted him to an adjunct teaching opportunity, made a recommendation, and, as they say, the rest is history. You'll learn more about his journey and the development of the Career Launch Method in the chapters that follow.

So, follow Sean's path, and start by figuring out what internships, research positions, and jobs might be a good fit for you. Follow his advice on how to transform your aspirations into reality. There is so much to gain by following the Career Launch Method. I believe that the skills you will develop in pursuit of your career goals will help you persevere through the challenging periods in your life and make the most of the opportunities that surround you. The confidence and courage you will gain will be substantial and will positively permeate the remainder of your life.

LAUNCH YOUR CAREER

From College to a Job You Want and a Career You'll Love

Are you seeking a fulfilling and meaningful career? Are you nervous about how to find one? Maybe you want a particular internship or job? Or, perhaps you are frustrated with the online search process? Maybe you lack clarity about what will fit you best despite researching different careers? If you answered yes to any of these questions, this book is for you.

If you are a career center leader, counselor, career coach, student success professional, or faculty, and you want to maximize your impact with students, this book is for you, too. As Jeremy and La'Tonya mentioned in their messages, this book can be easily integrated into for-credit courses and cocurricular programming.

Students, you carry a lot on your shoulders. You have to balance classes, homework, extracurricular activities, work, a social life, and taking care of yourself, all while preparing for your future career.

In my ten years of teaching, I've found that landing internships, research positions, and jobs is a huge source of stress for students. Most students approach their search by submitting applications online—a method that leads to an initial interview only 2% of the time.[1] Graduates who do find jobs are often underemployed; data shows that 42% of recent grads work in jobs that don't require a bachelor's degree.[2] Most students also know they will have student loan debt to repay. In 2019, the average student debt was $29,700.[3] Knowing these statistics and experiencing such a high rate of failure from online job applications creates anxiety for many. This confluence of realties is not great for students' mental health.

There's a better approach to a job or internship search that isn't so discouraging, a holistic process that doesn't focus on you sending your résumé into the black hole of online job postings hundreds of times. You see, research has found that 80% of jobs are filled through personal connections and are never posted on online job boards.[4] This means that there is an enormous hidden job market of which students are completely unaware. While some students may have family connections to help them get internships and jobs of interest, most students do not. I certainly didn't when I was in college.

My own career journey, my experience teaching and coaching students for more than a decade, and my research all have shown me that students who take intentional and strategic actions vastly outperform their peers in landing positions they want. I've used these experiences and research with thousands of students to create the Career Launch Method—a simple and actionable process that *any* student can use to land a position they target.

The Career Launch Method is a complete and detailed framework based on a key insight: the clearest path to landing internships and jobs is through building relationships with professionals in the industries and job functions where you want to work. These relationships are formed by setting up meetings with professionals—which I call "career conversations." At a minimum, career conversations will allow you to explore career fields, and often they will provide you with access to the hidden job market and get you hired.

The Career Launch Method works even if you don't have any existing industry connections. It works if you have below-average grades. It works regardless of your age, your experience, or your school's reputation. It works whether you attend a community college or a four-year university, or are pursuing a master's or PhD. It works for students in the United States and all over the world. It works if you're unsure about your career goals or if you're unsatisfied with the standard career options for graduates with your major. It works if you're an introvert who doesn't enjoy networking or if you have feelings of self-doubt or inadequacy. It can even work if the position you want doesn't currently exist.

Note: this book is written for current students, but the Career Launch Method works for recent grads—even for professionals of any age—with a few minor adjustments.

Throughout this book, I'll use the phrase "internships and jobs" to encompass the wide range of professional opportunities you might want to pursue. Whether you are looking for a competitive summer internship, a research position, a technical apprenticeship, a volunteer position, a grad school, a flexible remote job, or full-time employment after graduation—in any industry— the Career Launch Method is meant for you. It has worked for others like you who were pursuing a similar goal.

The frameworks in this book help address society's equity issue related to job search. Students with diverse backgrounds and identities face unique barriers in landing competitive internships and jobs. First-generation college students, international students, students with disabilities, and students from low–socioeconomic status households often face financial and/or cultural challenges and can lack the social capital needed for the career success they are seeking. The Career Launch Method is designed for students from all backgrounds, and it can help close these unfair opportunity gaps by teaching students how to create access to internships, jobs, and mentorships to launch their careers.

Since 2016, I've taught a career education class for first-generation college students at my university, and my social enterprise, Career Launch, has partnered with many organizations who focus on serving underrepresented students, beginning our partnership with the LEAD Scholars Program and the Hispanic Foundation of Silicon Valley. I am humbled to see the Career Launch Method help level the playing field and create social mobility for so many.

This book is based on my teaching at Santa Clara University, my guest lectures and workshops at other colleges and universities, my speaking engagements at conferences and career expos, and being one of the leaders of Career Launch. You can learn more at **www.careerlaunch.academy**.

Ever since the first class I taught, at the age of twenty-nine, I've known that teaching students how to explore careers, build social capital, and land the internships, research positions, and job they want is what I'm meant to do with my life. The past ten years have been an exhilarating journey, fueled by the success of my students. They tell me that the Career Launch Method not only helped them explore careers and land a position, but also helped them gain confidence and strategies to achieve their goals in other areas of life. Students frequently tell me that my class or a Career Launch program was one of the most impactful and valuable experiences in their life. It has been a privilege to speak at events across the country—not only to student audiences but also to career center professionals, faculty, and student success professionals—on how the Career Launch Method can be applied to for-credit classes and cocurricular programming.

The concepts in this book are also based on research. I teamed up with Barry Posner, best-selling coauthor of *The Leadership Challenge* and *The Student Leadership Challenge*. Together, we conducted a nationwide research study of students about students' career readiness, intentional networking, and internships. The results, which were published by the National Association of Colleges and Employers, have helped to validate the steps of the Career Launch Method and provide details on how career conversations lead to effective career exploration, increased social capital, and internships and full-time employment.

This book is a guide to creating a holistic job search strategy with actionable steps for building professional relationships from scratch in an effort to explore careers and land the jobs and internships you want. In the first chapter, I'll share the origin story of the Career Launch Method and how it transformed my career. In the following two chapters, I'll give you the crucial mindsets and attitudes that successful students adopt and I'll debunk eight common myths and mental blocks that hinder student success. Then, in chapter 4 I'll explain the six reasons why professionals will meet with you.

The majority of the book will be dedicated to the eight steps of the Career Launch Method, which demystifies how to use career conversations to land the internships and jobs you want. The method begins with some essential reflections to identify organizations you'd like to work for, then shows you how to translate this list of organizations into a list of professionals who can help your career exploration and job search. I'll show you the precise templates my students have used to successfully set up meetings with professionals and the step-by-step details of preparing for career conversations. Finally, we'll cover how to build long-lasting professional relationships and some the strategies you'll need to ace a job interview.

Each chapter includes concrete and simple actions. You'll discover strategic research tactics, detailed outreach templates, specific questions to ask, and confidence-boosting stories of students like you. Most importantly, the mindsets and strategies in the Career Launch Method will help you reflect on your values and achieve your goals, helping you create a meaningful career journey and life.

I am thrilled that you have chosen to read or listen to this book. If thinking about your future career or connecting with professionals gives you butterflies in your stomach or makes you nervous, you are normal. Almost all students have initial concerns about whether this method is right for them. I understand.

But I promise you—and I can state this confidently from my more than ten years of teaching students inside and outside of the classroom—that by the time you finish this book, your concerns will decrease and your confidence will increase. The student stories, mental and tactical frameworks, and practical actions in this book will give you a sense of control and agency over your career journey.

Here's how to most effectively read or listen to this book: If you are early in your college career or still in the process of deciding what internships, research positions, and jobs you'd like to pursue, I recommend that you read this book cover to cover. If you already feel confident about exactly which organizations you want to target, you can jump right to step 2 and then follow the remaining steps of the Career Launch Method.

Included with this book is the Career Launch Readiness Assessment, a tool that will give you customized scores, along with recommendations to take the next steps in your career readiness journey. The assessment will help you understand your strengths and areas for growth relative to five important competencies: career exploration, personal brand, relationship building skills, career search skills, and personal growth. Understanding where you are at in these areas will help you effectively apply the Career Launch Method to your life. I recommend you take the assessment before reading or listening to the rest of this book to establish a baseline of your compentecies. Then, take the assessment again after you finish book, which will provide you insights on your progress and growth. You can take the assessment three times. To access your survey, visit **go.careerlaunch.academy**.

I've also created the *Launch Your Career Workbook*, which contains key takeaways from the eight steps as well as space for you to answer reflection prompts and track your completion of each step. Visit **www.launchyourcareerbook.com** to learn more.

Each of the eight steps of the Career Launch Method contains several action items. If you focus on completing one action item at a time, you'll realize that this method is easy to implement and also very enjoyable because of the incredible possibilities that you can create for your career.

Congratulations on beginning this journey. Let's get started!

PART 1

How to Access
the Hidden Job Market

Most students are shocked when they discover that only 20% of all job opportunities are posted online.[1] And that doesn't mean that your school's online job platform posts only 20% of available jobs. It means *all of the job websites in the world, combined*, represent only 20% of available jobs, internships, and research positions. You might be skeptical of that statistic at first, as I was, but if you talk to professionals and look at research, you'll realize that it's true. People like to hire people they know or people their colleagues know. As a college student or recent graduate, your biggest challenge in the job search process is to become known by the right people at organizations where you want to work.

The next four chapters cover the strategies, mindsets, and knowledge you need to access the hidden job market. I'll discuss why the single most important thing you can do for your career is to apply a holistic approach to your job or internship search that includes proactive relationship building with professionals. The norm for students is to respond only to the opportunities put in front of them by their school or through popular websites, which is reactive. Students who are also proactive build more self-confidence, expedite their career exploration, and increase their chances for landing the positions they want. If you are seeking a job in a competitive industry, being proactive will differentiate you from an ocean of applicants and give you an advantage—oftentimes regardless of your GPA or prior experience.

The strategies in part 1 will show you the path to taking control of your career success and creating the mindset to achieve your goals.

◆ ◆ ◆ ◆

CHAPTER 1

The Origin of the Career Launch Method

Our deepest fear is not that we are inadequate. Our deepest fear is that we are powerful beyond measure. It is our light, not our darkness, that most frightens us. We ask ourselves, who am I to be brilliant, gorgeous, talented, fabulous? Actually, who are you not to be?

—MARIANNE WILLIAMSON

I was the first person on my mom's side of the family to go to a four-year college, and my dad was the first person in his family to do so, after he attended community college.

My life changed in the middle of my junior year. At the age of twenty, I hadn't given any thought to life after college. I was sitting in Professor Al Ferrer's sports management class at the

University of California, Santa Barbara, where I had transferred after attending a community college. Professor Ferrer told the class he had five summer internships with professional sports teams to hand out.

He asked the students, "Who's interested?"

As you might imagine with a class of sports management students, everyone's hand went up.

Professor Ferrer went on to say, "The only fair way I know to select who receives the internships is to reward the students with the best grades."

Upon hearing this, my shoulders slumped and I put my head down. I was far from being one of the best students. My grades consisted of mostly Bs and a few Cs.

But then Professor Ferrer continued, "If you are not one of the students with the best grades but you consider yourself a hard worker, come see me during my office hours and I will provide some tips to increase your chances of landing an internship with a professional sports team, even if you do not have any connections."

That line resonated with me because I considered myself a hard worker. My first job, during middle school, was delivering newspapers door to door at 4:00 a.m. In high school, I played sports and still worked as a cashier at the local pizza restaurant. In my first year of college, I started a four-year stint working for the kitchen knife company Cutco.

Although I had this work experience, I didn't have a résumé or cover letter. So I went home, found some examples on my career center's website, and quickly put together the documents. I showed up at my professor's office hours the next day, eager to learn about how to land an internship with a professional sports team.

Professor Ferrer told me that I needed to "zig when others zag." Applying to sports internships on the internet, well, that is what everybody does (zagging). I needed to take a different approach. I needed to have a holistic and proactive approach that included being targeted and strategic (zigging). I needed to do more than the typical student to stand out.

HOW TO ZIG WHEN OTHERS ZAG

That night, I made a list of the five professional sports teams that I would love to work for. Being a San Francisco Bay Area native, I targeted the San Francisco 49ers, Oakland Raiders, San Francisco Giants, Oakland A's, and Golden State Warriors.

Next, I made a list of the employees I thought could be strategically beneficial to me at each team. I realized that chief executive officers, chief financial officers, and chief operating officers don't hire interns. Neither do entry-level employees. At most reasonably sized organizations, people in director or manager positions hire interns. So I went to each team's website and online search engines (LinkedIn did not exist at the time), researched the names of all the directors and managers I could find, and added the names to a spreadsheet. I wasn't picky about finding the perfect department or division within the organization because I simply wanted to get my foot in the door.

On my spreadsheet, I added any additional information I could find about these people. For example, their email addresses, phone numbers, mailing address, and miscellaneous information such as educational background (and institutions), prior employers, favorite books, hobbies, and the like.

When I finished the spreadsheet, I narrowed my list to six directors at each of the five teams for whom I had enough information to reach out. I had a total of thirty business professionals who could potentially help me land an internship.

That was the easy part. Now it was time to figure out how to get any of these directors to engage with me. I thought to myself, I'm going to go old school. I'm going to send a cover letter and résumé via the U.S. Postal Service—snail mail. Not only that, but I also decided to print the documents on extra-thick card stock paper to showcase my extra effort. From my job experience with Cutco, I knew that little things can make a big difference in standing out from the crowd.

I purchased oversize envelopes (9 × 12 inches), because I knew that an oversize envelope was more likely to get noticed and opened than a regular-size envelope. I even thought about what type of pen I would use to handwrite the address and return address on the envelope. I knew a ballpoint pen would look puny, so I decided to use a Sharpie.

It took many hours over several days to create thirty envelopes with personalized cover letters to each director, but I felt that this was what it would take to land an internship in one of the most competitive industries in the world. I was very excited when I finished the project, and I dropped off the thirty envelopes at the post office. But was my excitement realistic? I knew that all thirty people wouldn't respond to me, but how many would? Two or three? Five or six? Ten or twelve?

After the first four days, I didn't have any responses.

After a week, still no responses.

After ten days, nothing. Not even an email acknowledging my gesture.

After fourteen days, I walked into Professor Ferrer's office and told him I had not received any responses. I was frustrated and depressed. The excitement that I had two weeks prior was long gone.

Professor Ferrer replied, "You know what you need to do next, right?"

I said no.

He said, "You need to call them."

I said, "Call them?" There was no way I could call these professionals. I was a pimple-faced, dyed-hair college student with average grades. Who was I to be intruding on their time? It would be rude of me to call them. Plus, I didn't know what I would say or what to do if they answered the phone.

Professor Ferrer said, "You're telling me that you can't dial someone's phone number and when they answer, say 'Hi, this is Sean O'Keefe, a student at UC Santa Barbara. I sent you a letter in the mail and I was wondering if you received it.' You can't say that?"

"Okay," I said. "Yeah, I can do that."

"If they say 'Yes, I did,' you then ask the person to advise you about the next step they would suggest for a student like you to take in obtaining an informational interview or internship. And if they say 'No, I didn't get your letter,' you say that you're interested in earning an informational interview or internship and ask if it would be okay to send them an email with a copy of your résumé and cover letter."

Despite feeling apprehensive, I brightened up and said, "Yeah, I can do that."

So, for the next three days, I called ten of the professionals on my list each day. I was hoping that someone would invite me into the interview process for a summer internship, or at least an informational interview.

Most people didn't answer the phone call and I had to leave voice mail messages. Some of the people who did answer told me I needed to contact the human resources department, some told me to call back in a couple months, and some told me there were no internships available in their department.

I received many rejections in response to my inquiries. In total, nobody invited me in for any kind of interview. I was dejected and feeling defeated. I gave serious thought to giving up. But the story is not over. Through my proactive outreach, by zigging, I was building a positive personal brand and reputation.

> When there's that moment of "Wow, I'm not really sure
> I can do this," and you push through those moments,
> that's when you have a breakthrough.
>
> —MARISSA MAYER

MOVING PAST REJECTION

After these rejections, I remembered my manager at Cutco, Stephen Torres, teaching me about the art of professional persistence. Professional persistence means that people who are asking for something should walk the line between being aggressive and avoiding follow-up. Continually contacting busy professionals is rude, but well-timed follow-up messages can show your commitment and increase your chances of success. Professional persistence alone will not earn you the position you want. You must demonstrate competence and confidence that you will excel in the job or internship you are seeking.

I decided I would send a follow-up email to each of the thirty professionals the next week, call again the week after that, and send another email the week after that. If somebody gave me a definitive no, then I would cross them off my list and stop reaching out to them.

I was extremely nervous during my calls and voice mails, pacing around my dorm room, but I tried to sound more calm and mature than I felt. I reminded myself that the worst thing that could happen was someone saying no to my requests.

I knew that landing an internship would increase my chances of landing a job after graduation, so I tried all sorts of strategies and tactics to get my foot in the door. I asked for informational interviews. I asked when and how the formal interview process for interns would occur. I explained how I would do a great job in the role, if given the opportunity.

And you know what?

It worked!

Ten weeks after beginning this process and mailing out thirty envelopes, I landed an internship. I would report to Lisa Wood in the marketing department of the Oakland A's!

Lisa told me that she had created the internship for me because of my efforts. I had convinced her that I could add value to her department. She told me that other candidates had reached out to her with better-looking résumés (higher GPAs, leadership positions with on-campus clubs, better experience, and so forth), but that because of my professional persistence and communication of competencies, she had felt compelled to create and design an internship for me.

Even though I grew up rooting for the San Francisco Giants, I was thrilled to have secured an internship with their rival Oakland A's. You can't be too picky when you are trying to land positions in highly competitive industries.

This was a pivotal point in my life. I had proven to myself, with help and advice from Professor Ferrer and Stephen Torres, that I could accomplish my lofty goal despite having no prior connections to the industry.

What an internship it was! Driving to the office meant driving to Oakland Coliseum, where the A's played their baseball games. I got to be the note taker during marketing meetings and to interact with fans during ball games. I also did lots of grunt work, like stuffing envelopes, which I did with joy.

At the end of the internship, I asked Lisa for, and received, a letter of recommendation that would be valuable for future job applications and interviews.

LEVERAGING ONE INTERNSHIP TO LAND ANOTHER

One week later, I was back in school at UC Santa Barbara. My summer internship with the A's gave me some credibility in the professional sports world, and I felt that I could use my momentum to make a compelling case to land another internship during my senior year. In my opinion, the greatest benefit of an internship is the opportunity to build personal relationships with people who make hiring decisions about full-time employees.

I now had industry experience and a letter of recommendation that I could strategically utilize as a reason to get back in touch with professionals from the other teams I had been contacting earlier in the year.

A San Francisco 49ers employee named Drew Casani in the Player Personnel Department had always taken my phone calls. It seemed like every time I called, he picked up. He would always begin, "Forty-Niners, this is Drew."

When I had first started reaching out to Drew, he told me that the personnel department hired an intern every winter to help out with the college draft. However, he said that this position was always filled by somebody close to the team's family (a son or daughter, niece or nephew, next-door neighbor, or similar), because the intern had access to highly confidential information.

At this point, I had spoken to Drew four or five times on the phone. I had a feeling I needed to create a stronger relationship with him. I told him about my experience with the A's and my letter of recommendation, and I asked him if it would be okay if I stopped by his office to put a face to my voice when I headed home for Thanksgiving. He agreed.

> *You have to do what you dream of doing, even while you're afraid.*
>
> —ARIANNA HUFFINGTON

As you can probably imagine, I put a lot of thought into how this face-to-face interaction would go. I planned out how I would greet him in the lobby, what kind of small talk I would make, what questions I would ask, and so on. (We'll cover these details later.) I also thought about how I would strategically finish the conversation by handing him a hard copy of my letter of recommendation from the Oakland A's, which would be inside the portfolio/notepad I would be carrying.

And that's exactly what I did. When we spoke in the lobby of 49ers headquarters, I could tell that Drew appreciated my effort to meet him in person. One of the questions I asked during our conversation was whether the team had filled the internship since our last conversation. He said they hadn't, and that *if* the team ended up in a situation where they didn't have anyone "close to the family," he would be sure to have the team interview me.

Even though this interview wasn't guaranteed, I was already nervous. I would potentially get a chance to speak to the team's leadership, and I didn't want to blow it. To prepare, I scheduled a meeting with a career counselor through my school's career center. The counselor was very helpful and recommended I schedule another appointment to utilize the center's mock interview technology so that I could record myself conducting a practice interview. I did, and it boosted my confidence for a potential interview with Drew's boss.

Fast-forward to January. I received a call from Drew saying that General Manager Terry Donohue would like to interview me for the winter internship.

I was excited beyond belief. Football was my favorite sport. Interning in the marketing department for the Oakland A's was amazing, but the possibility of interning for the San Francisco 49ers' Player Personnel Department was even more thrilling. I would be working directly for their coaches and scouts. Talk about a dream internship!

I thought about all the various aspects of successful interviewing, such as making small talk in the beginning, using stories to support answers to behavioral questions, maintaining good posture while seated, and making eye contact. I also studied 49ers history and statistics, but I was advised by my professor to not talk too much about being a fan of the team. It was much more important to convey how I would be effective in performing the duties of the internship.

On the day of the interview, there was no chance I was going to arrive late and jeopardize my opportunity. I planned to arrive thirty minutes before the interview and assumed the worst-case transportation scenario. There ended up being no issues, and I arrived seventy-five minutes early. Instead of checking in so early, I walked to a nearby coffee shop and reviewed my notes and the questions I had prepared. Twelve minutes prior to my interview time slot, I entered the 49ers building and checked in with the front desk. I was excited and nervous.

Drew came to the lobby to greet me and escorted me upstairs to a conference room where we spoke for about ten minutes until Terry Donohue, known as TD by his staff, was ready for us. Mr. Donohue's assistant escorted me into his enormous office. TD greeted me and asked me to sit in a chair in front of his oversize dark brown desk.

He told me I had been highly recommended by Drew and he asked some general questions about my schooling and experience interning with the Oakland A's. There were no trick questions or difficult questions about 49ers history.

In hindsight, I realize that the interview was simply a check on Drew's recommendation, because after about fifteen minutes TD started asking questions as if I were already hired. He asked me about the number of hours I preferred to work per week and what my ideal end date would be. And then he gave me a verbal offer for a paid internship!

I, of course, said yes, and then he had his staff prepare a written offer letter before I left the building. I signed and returned the letter the next day.

My dream internship got even better on my first day. I was told that I would have access to the weight room and have my own locker in the employee locker room. Additionally, I would be flying with team personnel to the NFL combine in Indianapolis. I'd have my own hotel room, free meals, and a close-up view to watch all the college players run the forty-yard dash.

Again, I had to pinch myself.

I was the "average grade" college student. I didn't have any prior connections to people at professional sports teams. But here I was with a football fan's internship of a lifetime. And it would not have occurred if I hadn't used the momentum from my A's internship as a reason to circle back with Drew.

GRADUATING WITHOUT A JOB

I knew my internships with the Oakland A's and San Francisco 49ers would increase my chances of earning a full-time position in professional sports after graduation, but I also knew that, like most things in life, it wasn't guaranteed. Professional sports teams do not operate like the accounting industry, in which summer interns frequently receive full-time offers for after graduation, soon after their internship ends.

During spring quarter of my senior year, I spent a lot of time trying, once again, to get job interviews with sports teams, but I was unsuccessful.

I graduated from UC Santa Barbara that June without a job.

I was pretty disappointed in myself. Why hadn't my efforts paid off with a full-time job?

My instincts told me that focusing solely on online applications was not going to land me a job I wanted, so I decided to double down on my approach of building relationships with professionals. I expanded my search from only sports teams to also include sports companies such as Nike, Under Armour, and Callaway Golf. In total, I conducted more than twenty career conversations and formal job interviews.

> *It is our choices . . . that show what we truly are, far more than our abilities.*
>
> —J. K. ROWLING

I still wasn't successful, and I was quickly running out of money. All I had was a bunch of rejection letters and emails. I had moved back home with my parents after graduation. They supported my desire for a job in sports, but they told me I could only live with them rent-free until September 1.

The end of summer came and I needed money to pay rent, so I took the first job I could get. This job turned out to be with Boise Cascade, a company that sells paper and office furniture. However, instead of settling into my role as a Boise employee and giving up entirely on the jobs I really wanted, I spent my lunch hours, nights, and weekends in pursuit of a position in sports, because I knew I would be more valuable to such an organization and would be more fulfilled personally.

One of the directors at the Oakland A's told me in August that the A's would be hiring three people for their business development team after the baseball season ended in late September/October. I knew I had a competitive advantage over other candidates because of my internships and the relationships I had built with employees from the marketing department who could recommend me.

On nights and weekends, I took time to reach out to these people. I made sure to express my enthusiasm for the business development role and I spent a lot of time thinking about strategic ways to stay in frequent contact with these people without annoying them. For example, in October, before the interview process began, I sent an email to the director of business development that included letters of recommendations from Lisa Wood, Stephen Torres, and Al Ferrer. Each letter affirmed my competence for the job. Subsequently, I spaced out follow-up emails and mailed handwritten notes to further express my qualifications and desire to join the business development team.

My proactive, strategic communication worked!

In November 2002, five months after graduation, I landed a full-time job in the business development department of the Oakland A's. I was responsible for finding businesses and organizations to purchase season tickets and luxury suites to utilize for client entertainment and employee benefits.

My hiring manager told me that my follow-up from August to November demonstrated my ability to communicate professionally and made it an easy decision to select me for one of the three open positions.

It took a lot of effort, but I accomplished my goal and launched my career.

◆ ◆ ◆ ◆

CHAPTER 2

Habits and Mindsets for Career Success

When there's a setback, someone with a fixed mindset will start thinking, "Maybe I don't have what it takes?" They may get defensive and give up. A hallmark of a successful person is that they persist in the face of obstacles, and often, these obstacles are blessings in disguise.

—CAROL S. DWECK

What is the biggest factor separating students who are successful in their job search from those who aren't? It's not grades, experience, or personality.

Students who land the internships and jobs they want consistently practice one key habit: they are *proactive*. Being proactive means that you take action to create opportunities for yourself.

When it comes to your career, being proactive is about building authentic relationships with professionals at the organizations where you want to work. It is the most effective way to achieve your goals.

To optimize success, you want to implement a holistic job search approach that includes both proactive and reactive strategies used simultaneously. Most students are only *reactive* when applying to jobs. They only respond to the opportunities rather than seeking to create them. Reactive methods include applying to positions through your school's online job portal, attending information sessions or career fairs, or submitting your résumé on job posting websites. All students should take advantage of these resources. While these strategies sometimes lead directly to jobs and internships, oftentimes it is hard to truly differentiate yourself. Reactive job search strategies should always be paired with the proactive strategies for a holistic approach that I'll teach you in the coming chapters.

THE POWER OF BEING PROACTIVE

Imagine that you are a hiring manager with two folders of résumés from job candidates. One folder contains two hundred résumés from random candidates who applied online, and the other folder has five résumés of candidates who were recommended by one of your coworkers. Which stack would you tackle first?[1]

As a student applying for internships and jobs, your goal is to be in the second folder. Employers like internal referrals. They also like candidates who are proactive in learning about the organization via networking with their employees. They know that candidates who exhibit such traits will likely show initiative and determination if they are hired. Employers also know that referrals will likely have a longer tenure at their organizations than candidates who simply apply online.

When thinking about the power of being proactive, there's a helpful concept called the law of attraction. It states that if you think positive thoughts, you attract positive emotions and events into your life, and if you think negative thoughts, you attract negative emotions and events into your life. Applying this idea of optimism to your career is a great first step, but you must pair your positive thoughts with intentional actions. Rather than simply *thinking* positively, you need to take concrete actions toward creating relationships and opportunities that don't currently exist. I call this "job search gravity." The more *proactive* steps you take toward career exploration and landing the internships or jobs you want, the more likely you are to cultivate job search gravity and get hired.

You have likely put a lot of effort into your education. Don't you owe it to yourself to maximize your chances to get the results you are looking for? I believe you do.

As the musician Drake says, "YOLO," or "You only live once." This phrase is often used to jokingly justify bad decisions, but it's also true in a literal sense. We all have one life to live. If you can't find the jobs you want through reactive approaches, don't settle. You have nothing to lose and everything to gain.

If you want to optimize your chances for success, you must incorporate a holistic approach that includes a proactive approach strategy like the Career Launch Method.

Focus on the process, not the outcome.

—JOHN WOODEN

One important thing to remember about being proactive is that you should focus on what you can control and avoid comparing yourself with others. Constantly immersing yourself in the news or social media is a recipe for becoming overwhelmed by things you cannot control. Similarly, comparing yourself with others can trigger negative emotions. It's easy to wish you went to *that* school, worked for *that* company, or had *that many* likes on your social media posts. Part of the key to career success (and to happiness more generally) is focusing on what you can control. What do you think about? How do you spend your time? Are you fully present or distracted when you are with people? Do you set goals to help you grow personally and professionally? Although so many things are out of your control, you have the power to make personal transformations and achieve a career goal by taking small steps. Learning to lead yourself is the first great challenge of leadership and of life.

My students often tell me that this shift to having a holistic and proactive mindset can be transformative in all areas of life. You can apply these concepts to friendships, fitness, family, schoolwork, spirituality, self-care, and more. Being proactive means taking action instead of overanalyzing, and it means volunteering to go first. You want to set realistic yet challenging goals, be accountable when you make a mistake, and take responsibility for things that are within your control. In short, a proactive mindset helps you create a fulfilling life.

Although being proactive about your career can produce anxiety, *not* taking action can do so just as well. A Career Leadership Collective survey found that 84% of students think about their career daily or weekly.[2] When students don't receive education or advice on such a top-of-mind issue, their mental health can be negatively affected. By utilizing the Career Launch Method throughout college, you can better link your academic efforts to life after school. You will create relationships with professionals who can help you when you figure out what you want to do, and who can help you face tough decisions and support you in your career journey, thus reducing your stress about your future career.

You don't need to have the rest of your life figured out today; you just need to be proactive and persistent in setting up career conversations to explore careers and create more opportunities for yourself. Realistically, you certainly shouldn't expect any single conversation to change your life. However, the likelihood that someone will provide valuable help on your job search—or even create a position for you—is much higher than you think. Once you realize the vast benefits of being proactive, you can overcome the mental hurdles that most students face.

If the idea of building relationships with professionals makes you nervous, you are normal. Proactively reaching out to people can be challenging for even the most extroverted students. Fortunately, it gets easier with practice—and with a step-by-step method to follow.

> *Careers aren't ladders, they're jungle gyms.*
>
> —SHERYL SANDBERG

THE JUNGLE GYM APPROACH TO CAREER SATISFACTION

From the time you enter preschool to the time you graduate college, you are on a fairly straight path. Elementary school leads to middle school, middle school leads to high school, and high school leads many students to college. Then when you finish college, you're in the "real world."

The "real world" is far different from the linear educational ladder. You are likely to work more than twelve different jobs between the ages of eighteen and fifty-two, and possibly quite a few more than that.[3] In today's quickly changing world, new jobs and industries are popping up all the time. The job type or industry you will really thrive in, or your "dream job," might not even exist yet!

There's a very good chance that your career won't be like climbing a ladder. It will be more like navigating a jungle gym, where you are moving in different directions, and no one direction is necessarily "better" than another. However, the core skills that you use from job to job will likely be similar. Critical thinking, communication, collaboration, adaptability, creativity, and professionalism will be important skills regardless of your job, function, or industry. This means that you should be open-minded about a wide range of possibilities for your future and know that there is no one path you must follow.

> *A rejection is nothing more than a necessary step in the pursuit of success.*
>
> —BO BENNETT

One key to navigating the jungle gym of your future is to treat every experience as a learning opportunity. Even if you find yourself manually entering numbers into a spreadsheet or washing dishes for a fast-food restaurant, you can still see your role as a chance to learn, add value, build your skills, and serve others. Knowing what you *don't* like can often be just as valuable as knowing what you do like, because you'll operate with more clarity and gratitude when you are in a situation you enjoy. If you're feeling stuck or worried about your transition from college to career, look for opportunities to develop a new skill set, or take on tasks that will help you grow.

It's normal to spend many years trying different job functions, industries, and career paths. In time, you will discover your passions and which jobs fit your skills and values. Even when you do get the job you really want, you probably won't enjoy it 100% of the time.

If and when you experience failure and frustration, I encourage you to reframe your perspective and view the experiences as learning opportunities and stepping-stones to success. You will get rejections. Some people won't respond to your proactive outreach. You might land an interview but not the position. You might end up in an internship or job you don't enjoy. You will make mistakes—and if you are like me, you will make *lots* of mistakes—in your work. This is all part of the learning process. Don't be too hard on yourself.

Rejection and mistakes don't mean *you* are a failure. The key is to develop the mental toughness to get back up when you fall and to try again. If you treat every project as a learning opportunity and do your best to be humble and add value, opportunities will come to you.

REVIEW AND REFLECT

- Applying a proactive approach to your job search will differentiate you from other candidates and help you build genuine relationships, which will benefit you for years to come. Having a holistic and proactive approach is more effective and enjoyable than just being reactive. It involves creating new opportunities for yourself rather than only responding to opportunities currently available. Are you embracing this approach?

- You're likely to work more than twelve different jobs in the first thirty years of your career. You can prepare to enter the rapidly changing workforce by treating every experience as an opportunity to learn, being persistent when you inevitably make mistakes or fail, and focusing on things that are within your control. How are you doing in these areas?

CHAPTER 3

Don't Believe These Common Misconceptions

The best way to not feel hopeless is to get up and do something. Don't wait for good things to happen to you. If you go out and make some good things happen, you will fill the world with hope, you will fill yourself with hope.

—BARACK OBAMA

Students often believe that they are inadequate or doomed for disappointment because of a series of misconceptions about what it takes to get an internship, research position, or job. Let's look at eight of the most common myths, along with the reasons why they are incorrect when applied to students like you.

MISCONCEPTION #1: YOUR INTERNSHIP OR JOB NEEDS TO BE RELATED TO YOUR MAJOR

Many students believe that once they choose a major or program of study, they are locked in to a narrow set of career paths—if you study accounting, you must become an accountant; if you study psychology, you must work in counseling or human resources. However, your major or program of study does not have to determine your long-term career path—or even your first job after college. Research shows that only 27% of college graduates in the United States end up in a career related to their academic major.[1] Other studies have found that many graduates take jobs that didn't even exist when they began college.

In addition, many students aren't even aware of the full range of jobs that relate to their major. For example, studying sociology prepares students to ask the right questions, conduct research, and analyze data. Any job title that includes the words "analyst" or "researcher" likely requires these skills, regardless of the organization or industry, but the job posting probably won't include the qualification "sociology majors preferred." Many majors and programs teach critical thinking skills and/or communication skills that will help you regardless of your career path.

Also, many students realize they aren't drawn to the typical career options available to graduates in their major. It is human nature to evolve and to have a change of interests from the time you choose a major or program of study to the time you finish school. Although this may make your job search more difficult, you can tell your story (during career conversations and interviews, as well as in your résumé and cover letter) to connect the dots between your interests, your studies, your skills, and your future ambitions.

One of my students, Gabriela, had dreamed for seven years of becoming a therapist. At the age of thirty, she immigrated to the United States and then earned a bachelor's degree in psychology. However, after shadowing a few therapists during her senior year, she realized that she wouldn't enjoy the work. She felt like her whole career plan had come crashing down. After graduation, Gabriela signed up for a few community college classes, registered for a Career Launch program through her school, and implemented the Career Launch Method to learn about, and find, other career options. Gabriela's career conversations led directly to her landing a research position she wanted.

Then, six months later, she decided to pivot once more and pursue a master's in gerontology. She again utilized a proactive strategy to build relationships with professionals at the graduate schools to which she was applying. Her efforts resulted in her receiving a verbal admission prior to the application process being finished.

Gabriela's success shows that you can change career paths and have success landing positions unrelated to what you study.

MISCONCEPTION #2: APPLYING TO JOBS ONLINE AND THROUGH CAREER FAIRS ARE THE ONLY/ BEST WAYS TO LAND INTERNSHIPS OR JOBS

Many students believe that positions advertised through their college's programs and events, or through online job websites, are the only jobs available to them. Again, all students should utilize these resources. If an organization you are interested in working for is attending your school's career fair, hosting a recruiting event, or interviewing on or through your campus, you should take full advantage of all these opportunities. And you should simultaneously be conducting career conversations with people in the specific departments of those organizations where you want to work, as a way to cultivate an internal advocate and separate yourself from all the other applicants applying online and/or who attend a career fair.

Remember, most internships and jobs are never advertised or posted online in the first place. By utilizing career conversations, you will have a twofold advantage over other students. First, utilizing career conversations in conjunction with submitting an online posting and attending career fairs will differentiate you. Second, utilizing career conversations with organizations that do not recruit at your school or have online openings can be your means to access the 80% of jobs in the hidden job market.

MISCONCEPTION #3: GPA IS EVERYTHING

It is true that a small number of graduate schools and companies require candidates to have a high GPA to be considered qualified for a position. Top law schools, medical schools, and some government agencies, along with the most selective accounting and consulting companies, often require applicants to have a GPA above 3.5 (or higher, like 3.8) to get noticed. However, these schools and companies represent a small fraction of all available opportunities.

Your GPA is just one indicator of your capabilities, though admittedly it is a quick way for organizations to sort through hundreds or thousands of applications. Most employers understand that your GPA doesn't fully represent who you are, but it's up to you to prove that to them. If you have a low GPA, you can still land an internship or job at a great organization—even at a competitive one.

The National Association of Colleges and Employers (NACE) has done research asking employers what attributes they look for in new graduates. The most important attribute was communication, with 82% of employers saying they highly value it. Close behind were problem solving, the ability to work in a team, and initiative.[2] These traits are all valued more highly than GPA by most employers. Don't be discouraged if you have a low GPA.

> *Don't be intimidated by what you don't know. That can be your greatest strength and ensure that you do things differently from everyone else.*
>
> —SARA BLAKELY

MISCONCEPTION #4: YOUR FIRST JOB DETERMINES YOUR LONG-TERM CAREER SUCCESS

Don't get me wrong; your first job can be an important stepping-stone to future opportunities. But it is not all or nothing—especially during a market downturn like the one that occurred due to the COVID-19 pandemic. Too many students believe that they are a failure if they don't get the perfect job right out of college.

In fact, it's very rare for students to get exactly the job they want right away, but this doesn't mean that their career ambitions are unattainable. Your first job doesn't lock you in to one industry, and it shouldn't determine your personal or professional identity. Treat your first job more as a learning experience than a prediction about your future. I have a friend, Zach, whose first job after finishing college was stocking shelves at a CVS pharmacy store; he now has a leadership position at Google.

Also, don't put too much pressure on yourself by comparing your choices and progress with that of your peers. Everyone's career path unfolds at a different pace. It's very common for students to work several different jobs before finding what a great fit means for them. Don't let your pace discourage you. The strategies in the Career Launch Method don't stop working after you graduate, so even if you don't like your first job, you can use career conversations to find new opportunities moving forward.

MISCONCEPTION #5: ASKING FOR HELP IS A SIGN OF WEAKNESS

Students are often told, by their families or others, that they should be able to accomplish everything all by themselves, and that independence is viewed as a sign of strength and intelligence. Many students (especially first-generation college students) have told me that they were raised in families where they were taught not to ask for help. But the reality, as the poet John Donne noted, is that no one is an island; we all need to rely on other people to thrive, collaborate, and find new opportunities. Other people have experiences and wisdom that you don't have, and you should recognize your inexperience and appreciate that no one expects you to have everything completely figured out at this stage in your life.

Asking for help is one of the smartest things you can do for your career. You will find that many professionals who have never met you are extremely willing to be of assistance just because you are a student asking for help. Professionals understand that the years during and immediately after college are some of the most uncertain in a person's career. Furthermore, the relationships that you build can be valuable for the rest of your life. Very seldom will opportunities come knocking at your door if you don't ask for help.

MISCONCEPTION #6: YOU DON'T HAVE ENOUGH EXPERIENCE TO LAND AN INTERNSHIP OR JOB

For many students, the most challenging internship or job to land is their first. Even if you have never had an internship or job, however, you still have valuable experiences that you can discuss with potential recruiters and employers. In addition to your coursework, perhaps you volunteer at a local organization, play a leadership role in your family, perform in the arts, play sports, or participate in various projects, individually or in a group. Each of these experiences will show employers your skills and character.

Students often mistakenly believe that employers are looking for more experience from students than they actually are.

Also, don't be discouraged if you don't meet every qualification on a job posting—this is especially true for internships. Research shows that the rate at which people are invited for interviews is no greater for candidates who meet all job description requirements than for those who meet more than half the requirements.[3] Studies have found that women and first-generation college students, especially, don't apply to jobs for which they don't meet *every* requirement. If you meet around half of the job requirements, you should apply. And you should simultaneously be creating relationships with professionals to develop an internal advocate and increase your odds of landing the position.

MISCONCEPTION #7: YOU NEED TO PLAN YOUR FUTURE CAREER BEFORE YOU GET STARTED

Wrong. The truth is you don't need to have a clear idea of what career you want to pursue for the rest of your life when you begin building relationships or searching for internships. One of the major advantages of career conversations and internships is that they can help you discern what types of jobs you might want in the future. Learning from others about what you *don't* like is just as valuable as learning what you *do* like. If you have five different job types, industries, organizations, or graduate schools you're interested in, you likely don't have time to earn an internship in each area to help discern which you prefer. Though you can expedite your discernment process by learning vicariously through career conversations.

You should never wait until you're certain to begin networking and applying, because you'll never be fully certain. It's also likely that through networking and completing internships, you'll be surprised by what you gravitate toward. The bottom line is that you should never let your uncertainty prevent you from taking action.

MISCONCEPTION #8: YOU'RE NOT GOOD ENOUGH, OR YOU'RE NOT WORTHY

Maybe you've been told by family, friends, or teachers that you can't do something. Maybe no one in your family or community works in the industry in which you aspire to work. Maybe you have a DUI or similar infraction on your record. Maybe you have to work two or three minimum-wage jobs just to make ends meet. Maybe you've applied to more than one hundred jobs online and never even obtained an interview. All of these are challenging roadblocks, to be sure, but none of them make you unworthy of a career that you love.

Everyone faces different challenges in their career journey, but if you persevere with the right strategy, you can overcome the odds and get a job you'll love. It may take time, courage, and persistence, but you can do it. If you have persevered through difficult circumstances in your life, you likely have unique skills and mindsets that organizations will definitely value. You will need to learn how to tell your story so that future employers recognize your skills and character.

REVIEW AND REFLECT

- Your major, experience, and GPA shouldn't hold you back from pursuing your career goals. You also don't need to have your whole career planned out or worry that your first job will limit your future career options. Additionally, know that asking for help is a crucial aspect of career success. Which misconception do you identify with most?

- Many students have objections to being proactive in their careers and are hindered by a series of false beliefs about what it takes to land an internship or job. Know that right now, despite your self-doubt, you are good enough to land an internship or job, and you are worthy of professionals' time. Take a moment to reflect on this.

CHAPTER 4

Professionals Will Want to Meet with You

To overcome our challenges, we need to find the courage to ask for help.

—SIMON SINEK

When I tell students about the importance of building relationships through career conversations, they often wonder why any professional would want to meet with them. Why would a professional who has achieved some level of career success bother to speak with a student?

There are all sorts of reasons why professionals say yes to meeting with students.

Imagine this hypothetical situation. You have ten to forty years of work experience and enjoy the job you have. One day, you receive a polite and professional email from a student, expressing admiration for your experiences and wondering if you have twenty minutes to share your insights about their questions about life after college. If you had the time, wouldn't you say yes to that student?

SIX REASONS WHY PROFESSIONALS MEET WITH STUDENTS

Relationships with professionals will help you explore careers, earn internships and jobs, cultivate mentorships, build friendships, encounter opportunities to serve others, and tap into new communities and networking circles. To realize these benefits, you have to understand that professionals (both those you have some existing relationship with, however slight, and complete strangers) will want to meet with you.

Here are six reasons why professionals meet with students:

1. **Paying it forward.** Professionals are often enthusiastic about repaying the support they received in their younger years.

2. **Empathy toward your situation.** Professionals remember what it was like to be a student with no job and few to no connections, and they often like to help people like you.

3. **They find it flattering that you want to learn from them.** By initiating a career conversation, you are communicating to the professional that their experience is valuable and that they have something important to teach you.

4. **They like to talk about themselves.** Some people just really enjoy talking about themselves and about their career journey. Others may welcome the career conversation as a needed break from their day-to-day responsibilities.

5. **It makes them look good to others.** Some profession-als report that they agree to meet with students because it makes them look good to their spouse, kids, friends, and coworkers.

6. **They are involved in recruiting.** Even if someone isn't a recruiter or hiring manager, they may still be involved in the recruiting process for roles at their organization. If so, meeting you could help them fill a position on their team.

I hope that understanding these reasons gives you confi-dence in reaching out to professionals. But don't expect that any particular person will meet with you. You must be respectful and considerate in your outreach. More on that in step 4. And even then, you will not always get a yes. It's a numbers game. To quote Jack Canfield, "Some will. Some won't. So what. Someone else is waiting."

Keep in mind that alumni from your school and profession-als with similar backgrounds, majors, or programs of study are more likely to accept your request out of a sense of school spirit or commonality. But the reasons above apply to any professional you may want to contact.

Again, not everyone will say yes to your requests, but you'll likely be surprised by how gracious and welcoming profession-als will be in response to requests for career conversations if you follow the Career Launch Method.

> *If you are successful, it is because somewhere, sometime, someone gave you a life or an idea that started you in the right direction. Remember also that you are indebted to life until you help some less fortu-nate person, just as you were helped.*
>
> —MELINDA GATES

Consider the story of one of my students, Lydia.

Lydia was raised by immigrant parents who emphasized the value of hard work and humility. She studied accounting in college and worked hard to get good grades, but she wanted to expand her career aspirations beyond the traditional accounting path. Between her junior and senior years, Lydia had earned an internship with Big Four accounting firm PwC, which resulted in an offer of a full-time job upon graduation. But instead of coasting through her senior year, Lydia decided that she wanted to get an internship in a smaller, more entrepreneurial environment.

In my class, Lydia heard a story about Tom Chi, an entrepreneur and investor who helped cofound Google X, the secretive research and development unit within Google. She admired Tom's determination and accomplishments, so she followed the steps of the Career Launch Method and set up a career conversation with him. Tom agreed to meet with her by video chat or in person. Lydia didn't own a car and didn't have much money, but she decided it would be worth taking public transportation to have the meeting in person.

On the day of the meeting, Lydia took the train to San Francisco for the conversation. Tom answered Lydia's questions about his experiences and career options, and they made a special connection over their mutual first-generation college student status and Asian heritage. After that conversation, Lydia sent an email and handwritten note thanking Tom for his time and insights.

A couple months after this initial conversation, Lydia followed up with Tom, thanking him again for the conversation and asking him about any internship opportunities he might know about. Tom responded saying that her timing was perfect and that he was looking for someone with accounting knowledge like Lydia's to help build accounting processes for a start-up in which he was a lead investor. Because Lydia had created a relationship with Tom through her initial career conversation, she was quickly hired for an internship. She was ecstatic; she created a life-changing internship from scratch!

Lydia's story shows that even the most accomplished professionals are often willing to meet with students who are genuine, respectful, and persistent—and then willing to offer them a job! Here's what Tom shared with me about the experience from his perspective:

> Lydia reached out to me out of the blue. I did not know her. The email was written professionally and it had an inquisitive sense to it, and I was open to taking the meeting. In the meeting, she presented herself really well and asked smart questions. After her follow-up a month later and consulting with my team, we decided to offer her an internship. And within a couple weeks of her starting, she was a contributing member of the team. I think our team got a lot and she got a lot from the months we worked together.

You can find Tom's video testimonial, along with those of other professionals speaking about their experience with students who have utilized the Career Launch Method, at, **www .careerlaunch.academy/employers**.

REVIEW AND REFLECT

- Professionals meet with students for many reasons. First and foremost, everyone receives help and mentorship from others, and professionals like to pay forward to the younger generation the help they themselves once received. Has your view about professionals' willingness to meet with you changed?

- Professionals find it flattering and energizing to be asked to meet with a student and discuss their career path. Being a student is an asset, not a roadblock, when building relationships with professionals. Realizing this, what will you start doing?

PART 2

The Career Launch Method

This section goes into detail on the eight steps of the Career Launch Method, the process that my students have used for more than a decade for career exploration and to land internships, research positions, and jobs they want. The Career Launch Method shows you how to use career conversations to learn vicariously about career options, build relationships with professionals, and access new opportunities.

My research with professor Barry Posner showed that more than 90% of students who completed career conversations (aka informational interviews) received an internship or research position![1] Other findings also highlight the connection between career conversations and internships, including the following:

- Students who conducted at least one career conversation during college were *four times more likely to earn an internship* than students who did not conduct career conversations.

- Students who conducted at least one career conversation during college were *eight times* more likely to have completed *two or more internships*.

- Students' *self-confidence* and confidence in building relationships *increased* directly with the number of career conversation conducted as well as the number of *internships* completed.

- First-generation college students who conducted career conversations via cold networking (reaching out to professionals they did not know beforehand) were *four times more likely* to have their internships turned into jobs than first-generation students who did not do cold networking.

Perhaps most telling, students' most common response to the question *What piece of career readiness advice do you wish you knew sooner?* was *How to network and conduct career conversations*.[2] The eight steps outlined in the following chapters will show you exactly what you need to do to maximize your chances for success.

Keep in mind that the Career Launch Method is best practiced *before* you need an internship or job. It can work *during* your job search, too, but your chances are greater if you start early, simply for career exploration purposes. A modified version of the method also works *after* you land a job, to build relationships with your new coworkers, to land your next role, or to change industries or career paths.

Students who begin proactive outreach to professionals early on put themselves in an excellent position to land the job they want upon graduation or certificate completion. Plenty of students have also used the Career Launch Method years after they graduate to land new jobs. These strategies and tactics can be adapted to meet your career goals for years to come.

◆ ◆ ◆ ◆

Discernment—Prioritize the Organizations You Want to Work For

To be yourself in a world that is constantly trying to make you something else is the greatest accomplishment.

—RALPH WALDO EMERSON

As a first-generation college student, Marieli entered college without giving her career much thought. In high school, she had been focused on applying for scholarships and getting into a university but hadn't spent much time reflecting on what type of career she wanted. Most people she knew in her small town worked in the hospitality industry, so she imagined she would do the same. She knew some of her broad interests, such as writing, public speaking, and hands-on problem solving, but she wasn't sure how those interests would translate into a major in college or a job afterward.

"I simply assumed my college education would grant me instant employment and a secure job after graduation," Marieli said. "Little did I realize that vocational exploration and effective job searching requires being proactive, persistent, and even courageous."

Marieli first chose to study in the school of arts and sciences, but she later switched to civil engineering. She worried that this decision would pigeonhole her into one kind of job for her whole life. She worried that she would end up in a stagnant career that wouldn't motivate her to jump out of bed every morning. She worried that her income wouldn't be enough to support herself or her family. At Santa Clara University, Marieli often heard about friends landing internships based on their family connections, which left her feeling like she would be unlikely to find a job she loved.

Marieli took my career education class during her sophomore year. She learned that, in many cases, when it comes to job searching, *who* you know matters more than *what* you know. She realized that by talking with professionals and building relationships, she could take ownership of crafting her career trajectory, learn about different career paths, and land internships to gain practical experience.

On the first day, I asked each student to write down ten organizations where they might want to work after college. Marieli's mind went blank. She glanced around the room and saw her classmates writing down prominent companies like Netflix, Microsoft, and Facebook, but those well-known brands didn't feel right for her. Rather than writing the first ten organizations that came to mind, Marieli spent a few days researching

STEP 1 | 2 | 3 | 4 | 5 | 6 | 7 | 8

organizations online and tried to picture herself in the organizations she researched. She selected three job areas she wanted to learn more about: construction, environmental engineering, and becoming a civil engineering professor. Next, she simply did an online search for each area (for instance, "top construction companies in the San Francisco Bay Area"). She looked into the organizations' culture, mission, employee reviews, and examples of past projects. Did her values align with the apparent values of the organization? Would she be interested in their work? Did she care about their mission?

Starting with an initial list of more than twenty companies and various job functions, she slowly eliminated some that didn't have the attributes she was looking for. Marieli also asked close friends and family members if they could imagine her working in some of the roles she had chosen. Her final list of ten ranged from construction and environmental engineering companies to organizations in the nonprofit sector and in academia.

Marieli's reflection on her values and research on her dream companies ended up paying off. Using the steps of the Career Launch Method, Marieli began having career conversations with a variety of professionals. She overcame her self-doubts and became comfortable introducing herself to people she had never met. Marieli leveraged her new confidence to reach out to the manager of a construction company, which led to a career conversation. The conversation went really well and resulted in a job shadow experience and then an interview for an internship that wasn't posted online. Very quickly, Marieli landed an internship as a field engineer at this company! The internship ended up being a great experience for her post-sophomore-year summer and taught her valuable lessons about the "real world."

"My biggest tip would be to use your sophomore year to start creating relationships with professionals," Marieli shared. "I was able to gain clarity on my strengths and interests based on the career conversations and the internship. I always had an open mind when trying something new and tried to eliminate all expectations and prejudgments. Listen to yourself and your gut, not external factors, to determine. whether you're curious and excited to learn about certain job functions or particular organizations."

Marieli's story shows the power of discernment—making wise decisions based on reflection, research, and experimentation by taking action. There are an unlimited number of career paths available, but often students only consider careers they see in their family, their community, the media, or careers related to their major or program of study.

Career discernment is the process of identifying the suitability of particular job types and career paths and deciding which to pursue first. The two most critical parts of discernment are experiences and reflection. Experiences could include career conversations, projects, attending informational sessions, participating in competitions, job shadowing, internships, and so on. These are all great ways to learn, whether firsthand or vicariously, about job types and careers.

Just as important, though, is to intentionally make time to reflect on your experiences—deep, thoughtful reflection that pays attention to small details and your emotions. In a world that competes for your limited attention, discernment is countercultural. It means you ponder your actions and become more aware of the gentle nudges that give you insight into what decisions to make next.

Discernment isn't a one-time activity. It is not an item on a to-do list that you can check off and forget about. Ideally, discernment is an on-going process that involves reflecting on yourself, your experiences, and the world around you. A wide variety of activities can help you discover a career you'll love: journaling, conversations with trusted friends, spending time in nature, and life experiences. You should also engage with your college's career center and inquire about free assessments you can take to learn about how your strengths and personality relate to careers. When life gets busy, it's easy to push off some of these activities. One way to ensure that you are periodically returning to discernment questions is to mark off time in your calendar, perhaps on a quarterly basis, and set reminders. There's no correct schedule; you may go through intense periods of discernment while in college but only need to return to the big questions several times per year when you are working in a job you enjoy, or when there are major changes in your circumstances (such as considering a mortgage, a partner, or a family).

Remember, you do not need to decide on your lifelong career while you are in college. At this stage of your life, learning what you *don't* like is just as valuable as learning what you *do* like. For Marieli, her internship made her realize that she did not want to pursue a traditional civil engineering job right after college. Don't put pressure on yourself to decide what you want to do forever. Just keep taking action and use your experiences, skills, and reflection to help you move forward in the right direction. Also, don't be afraid to enlist people with whom you are close to help you think about your discernment journey. Having conversations with career counselors, professors, close friends, mentors, or family members can be a great way to get an outside perspective on what jobs and career paths would suit you.

Your action item for this step will be to make a list of ten organizations where you think you *might* want to work. As you create your list, spend some time thinking about the discernment questions and topics in this chapter. **But don't overthink your list; you can always come back later and add or change the organizations you've selected.** The Career Launch Method is about taking action, so don't overanalyze this step!

After finishing this chapter, take thirty minutes to write down as many organizations on your *initial* top

ten list as you can. If you don't finish your list, make time to do so in the next two or three days.

> *I am learning every day to allow the space between where I am and where I want to be to inspire me and not terrify me.*
>
> —TRACEE ELLIS ROSS

KEY TAKEAWAY #1: DISCOVER YOUR IKIGAI

The first step to launching your career isn't to look at what opportunities are available in the world; it's to look inside, at yourself. Students often want to skip over this step and jump into applying to big-name organizations. But self-awareness is essential to finding jobs that you will find meaningful and that will contribute to your growth.

One helpful concept to begin the discernment process comes from the Japanese concept of *ikigai* (pronounced *ee-key-guy*), which means "a reason for being." Your ikigai is the sense of purpose, meaning, and well-being that arises from living a fulfilling life. Why do you get out of bed in the morning? Ikigai is your answer.

The concept of ikigai has existed in Japan for centuries, but it became popular in Western culture due to Dan Buettner's research on "blue zones." Buettner studies areas like Okinawa, Japan, where many people live to be more than one hundred years old. As figure 1 shows, your ikigai lies at the intersection of four different dimensions. What you love to do intersects with what you are good at and generates passion. What you love to do also intersects with what the world needs, to create a sense of mission. What the world needs and what you can be paid for create a vocation. What you can be paid for and what you are good at show you potential professions. Along with your sense of

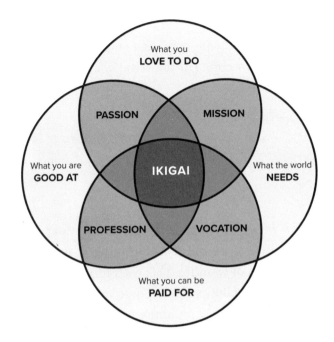

FIGURE 1. *Discovering your ikigai.*

identity, these intersecting and overlapping dimensions can help you discover your life purpose.

You may be thinking, *Why do I need to figure out why I exist when all I want is an internship and then a job to be able to pay off my student loans?* Or, more pessimistically, you may be thinking, *I'll be lucky if I'm able to get* any *job. There is no way I can get a job I really want.*

The main reason—or one of the main reasons—you decided to go to college in the first place probably was to get a good job. Take the time now for discernment. You don't want to wake up one day and wonder, *What if . . . ?*

You can always default to just finding "any job" to help you pay the bills. But taking the time for discernment now can make a difference in your career satisfaction and life fulfillment for decades to come. Finding meaningful work can be a challenging journey, but your odds will increase if you begin with an honest assessment of four sections of the ikigai chart: *mission, profession, vocation,* and *passion.*

> *Sound judgement, with discernment is the best of seers.*
>
> —EURIPIDES

Your *mission* is where what you love to do meets what the world needs. Reflect on the most meaningful projects, activities, or experiences of your life. This is an important exercise, so don't rush your thinking process. These experiences will likely share common elements: community with other people, dedication to a cause bigger than yourself, and a sense of immersion in which time flies by. Many people want their careers to serve other people or to make the world a better place. Others want to make a difference with how they use their leisure time, earn extra money, or interact with their friends and family.

Second, your *profession* is formed by the combination of what you're good at and what you can be paid for. Many students have an easier time answering the first question, about what they're good at, than they do the second, about what they can be paid for. One of the beautiful parts of today's economy is that the range of possible professions is greater than it has ever been. Online research and career conversations can help open your mind about the range of career options available, but you still have to figure out what you're good at, and this insight comes through reflection, experimentation, and conversations with people who know you well. Think about the following questions:

STEP 1 2 3 4 5 6 7 8

- What skills do you currently have?

- How would close family, friends, or mentors describe your strengths and skills?

- What activities are so energizing that they make you lose track of time?

- What job roles or careers most interest you now?

- What skills would you like to learn?

- Whom do you admire? Why?

> *Discernment is not a matter of simply telling the difference between right and wrong; rather, it is telling the difference between right and almost right.*
>
> —CHARLES HADDON SPURGEON

Third, your *vocation* is a pairing of what the world needs with what you can be paid for. The term "vocation" refers to a career that you are dedicated to and passionate about. Not everyone will find their vocation through their job, and this isn't necessarily a problem. Perhaps an aspiring musician prefers to work full time at a restaurant to pay the bills and to dedicate her spare time to creating music. Someone else can find an overlap between their career and financial success and helping the world through philanthropy. The vast majority of students do not find a job that fulfills their vocation right out of college; discovering a vocation is a lifelong process that will involve numerous twists and turns. But it's never too early to start thinking about your future impact or the legacy you want to leave behind.

Importantly, vocation requires intrinsic motivation. Our modern world encourages pursuits driven by extrinsic motivation, such as looking good on social media, accumulating money, owning a fancy car, and wearing expensive clothes. I was extrinsically motivated upon graduating from college. All I cared about was how much money I could make and the brand name of the organization I worked for. It wasn't until several years past graduation that I cared less about benefiting myself and much more about positively impacting others.

It's easy to fall into the trap of selecting jobs based solely on extrinsic factors like money and what other people will think about you. Do an honest self-assessment. How do you relate to the career options you are pursuing? Do you feel that you're led by inspiration or by fear? Are you driven primarily by intrinsic or extrinsic motivation? It's not necessarily bad to be motivated by extrinsic factors like money or prestige, but these things are unlikely to lead to true fulfillment.

Many people's vocation comes out of their difficult life experiences and tough times. For some, their mess becomes their message. Rather than asking, *Why did this or that happen to me?*, ask instead, *What can I learn from this experience?* Certainly, many people face oppression and suffering that makes pursuing a vocation challenging. But perhaps your experiences—positive and negative—can help you be of greater service to others with similar experiences going forward.

> *I've come to believe that each of us has a personal calling that's as unique as a fingerprint—and that the best way to succeed is to discover what you love and then find a way to offer it to others in the form of service, working hard, and also allowing the energy of the universe to lead you.*
>
> —OPRAH WINFREY

STEP **1** 2 | 3 | 4 | 5 | 6 | 7 | 8

Finally, your *passion* is a combination of what you love to do and what you are good at. Some students find frequent overlap in these two areas, since people often enjoy activities that allow them to add value and receive recognition. However, the vast majority of college students don't know what they are passionate about in terms of career because they haven't had enough life or work experiences to have clarity about what they most care about—and especially about how this translates into a possible job or career. The good news is that you will realize your passions over time. Discernment can accelerate your discovery.

Consider this: In a hypothetical world in which finances were not an issue and you could do anything with your time, what would you do? What gets you excited? If you have a hard time answering these questions, don't worry, because most people, not just students, have a tough time answering these questions. It's rare for students to have 100% clarity about their life direction.

Spend some time thinking about your ikigai. For the moment, all you need is a starting place. Don't worry about trying to have it all figured out. Remember, career paths are very seldom linear. These are big questions, and you likely will be thinking about them for years and even decades to come.

> *Sometimes you have to look back in order to understand the things that lie ahead.*
>
> —YVONNE WOON

KEY TAKEAWAY #2: EVALUATE THE TEN FACTORS THAT MATTER IN A JOB

To gain additional self-awareness, to gaining self-awareness, you need to know which elements matter to you most in a job. Many students fall into the trap of evaluating a job along only one dimension, such as thinking that a job will be awesome because it's at a big-name company, organization, or institution. Did you know over 90% of private-sector employers with more the 20 employees are small to mid size organizations (less than 1,000 employees)?[1] There is nothing wrong with working for a big-name organization. There are wonderful big-name organizations that provide excellent jobs and career opportunities. The point is to look more holistically at potential opportunities.

Below are the ten factors that I've found, through reviewing the literature and personal experience, to influence success and happiness in a job. There is no order to this list, and there is no right or wrong order in which factors should be prioritized. Take some time to consider how significant each of these characteristics is to you personally, and then incorporate your priorities into your research into organizations where you want to work.

1. **Job function.** Will you be able to use your skills and interests in the job role? Will you find the work meaningful? Will you enjoy performing the duties of the position?

2. **Learning/growth opportunities.** Can you work on exciting projects? Are there advancement opportunities? Will the job help you build valuable skills?

3. **Relationship with supervisor.** How closely will you work with your supervisor? Do you value that person as a leader?

4. **Time commitment.** How many hours per week will you be working, and are you okay with that? Will the position require you to travel? If so, is that something you want?

5. **Organizational culture and values.** How do employees describe the leadership, environment, values, mission, and ethics of the organization? How does the organization contribute to society? Does the organization embrace diversity, inclusion, and equity?

6. **Organization size.** Is this a multinational corporation? A local small business? A health clinic? A school district? A regional organization? A start-up? Is it likely to change in size, to get smaller or larger? Consider the pros and cons of working for different-size organizations; what is best for you?

7. **Industry.** Do you value the industry or particular organizations more than the job function you will be performing, or vice versa?

8. **Geography.** Where do you desire to live? Is it important to work near a company office or facility? Will you need to commute or relocate? Can you work remotely?

9. **Risk/security.** What sort of job security does the organization provide? Is the organization in a stable financial position? Is this a stable industry? Do you prefer stability or like the possible upside that comes with risk?

10. **Compensation.** How much will you be paid? Hourly or salary? Bonuses? Stock options? Commission? What benefits will be provided, and which are most important to you?

The degree of importance of these ten factors can change throughout your life and can vary widely from one person to the next. For example, my sister used to put a premium on *time commitment* and *geography*. She didn't want to work more than forty hours per week and she was determined to work and live in a beach city. My values were different. I was okay with working fifty to seventy hours per week in my twenties. *Industry, compensation*, and *learning/growth opportunities* were most important to me at that time. I wanted to work in the sports industry, have the opportunity to earn a leadership position at a young age, and have a role that provided lucrative commissions and bonuses. My priorities have changed over time, as yours most likely will, too.

Take a few minutes and consider each of these elements. Assign a score to each, from zero to 100, based on how important each is to you. In addition, write down some notes on what you are looking for within each of these categories. Some of these traits are easy to discover through online research into an organization, while others will require career conversations with current or former employees to get an inside perspective. This information will help you identify an initial list of *ten* companies or organizations where you would like to work.

REVIEW AND REFLECT

- Take a deep breath. Remember that you don't need to figure out what job you will do for the rest of your life. You can take small steps that are well within your control to put yourself on track to get a job you want. And it's okay if you accept an internship, apprenticeship, or job that isn't a great fit. Many successful people started in positions they didn't enjoy and then moved on to something different that became their life's true path.

- Schedule time on your calendar to reflect on your skills, values, goals, and career aspirations. For example, you might set aside an hour every other week to journal, have a call once per month with a mentor, or take two hours every quarter or semester to reflect on what's happened and what actions you'll take or behaviors you'll adopt going forward.

- If you feel a little stuck in your discernment, set up a meeting or video call with a trusted family friend, mentor, professor, career counselor, or someone else who knows you well and might have ideas about which career options could suit you.

ACTION ITEMS

1. Spend some time reflecting on the ikigai questions and writing down your answers in a journal. Then think about how your answers to these questions can generate useful ideas for identifying potential career options:

   a. What am I good at?
   b. What do I love to do?
   c. What can I be paid for?
   d. What does the world need?

2. Return to the "Ten Factors That Matter in a Job" section. Write down how important each element is for you and note any of your preferences in the different areas. Also take note of which areas you want to learn more about during career conversations. Make some notes about the three to five factors that are most significant to you at this moment.

3. Take time to research organizations that fit the characteristics you are looking for in a job.

4. In the next two to three days, create an initial list of ten companies, organizations, or institutions where you would like to intern or work. Don't overthink this! You can make changes and additions later.

Strategic Research— Discover Professionals Who Can Be Helpful to You

Discernment and planning cannot be separated. By planning without discerning, we are administrators. By discerning without planning, we are dreamers.

—FATHER ARTURO SOSA, SJ

Garibaldi had one thing on his mind as he graduated: to get his green card application sorted out as quickly as possible. After attending college in the United States, he was eager to return to his hometown of Jakarta, Indonesia. A green card, however, would allow him to return to the United States and secure employment.

He submitted his application and waited to hear from the U.S. embassy. He knew there was a chance his application would be denied. As a backup plan, he thought it would be wise to explore career options in Indonesia.

Garibaldi had always been interested in real estate, but he didn't have any connections in the industry. He began researching firms, small and large, but with a focus on searching for smaller real estate firms in Jakarta. During his research, he found a publication that listed awards given to the top companies in the commercial real estate industry. This awards list gave him several companies to explore further.

Garibaldi was unable to find personalized information on LinkedIn or the organizations' websites, so he would either guess people's email addresses or use the general contact email offered on websites. Of his five initial emails, two bounced back and two received no response. But one person did respond, and that contact was William, the thirty-one-year-old CEO of an up-and-coming boutique real estate firm. Garibaldi arranged to have a career conversation and William suggested meeting at a local restaurant.

At one point in the conversation, William turned to Garibaldi and said, "You know, you could work for us. We are actually looking for more outgoing, hardworking people in our company."

Garibaldi was surprised and didn't know how to respond. He wanted to say yes, but he knew that if his green card application was approved, he intended to move back to the United States in a few months. Under these circumstances, he felt that it would be unfair to work for such a short period of time. He politely declined the invitation to talk further about a job. The next morning, Garibaldi sent William a thank-you email expressing his gratitude for the meeting and the overture.

Two months later, in March 2020, Garibaldi received an email from the U.S. embassy explaining that his green card interview had been canceled due to the COVID-19 pandemic. He was quite disappointed. After a few days of reflection, Garibaldi realized that although he couldn't control what had happened, he could decide what to do next.

He reached back out to William, explained the visa denial, and asked if there might still be an opportunity to work at the firm. To his delight, William told him that the company was still looking to add to their team and asked Garibaldi if he could interview with them the next week. Shortly afterward, Garibaldi was offered the job.

For Garibaldi, this experience was validation of the Career Launch Method. "It works wherever you are in the world." Garibaldi said. "Even though career conversations may not be common in countries such as Indonesia, it did not stop me from trying. My recommendation is that every student should use the method and see where it takes them. You never know. Expect some setbacks and rejections, but do your best, give it everything you've got, and follow all the steps. It can change your life."

Garibaldi showed resilience during his job search, and his strategic research to identify people like William was key to his landing a job he wanted.

The exercise of creating a list of your top ten organizations in step 1 is a precursor to taking the next step. *As you move from step 1 to step 2 of the Career Launch Method, it is important to realize that it's okay to be unsure about your career path.* Discernment requires active experimentation and learning what you do and do not like. The key is to continually gain new experiences and to reflect on those experiences. Then take more action and repeat the cycle.

Whether or not you have clarity about your vocation, completing the action items in this chapter will help you explore career options and get you closer to obtaining the internships or jobs that you want—or that you think you might want. The objective of step 2 is to identify professionals who can help you achieve your short-term and long-term career goals. Utilize the Strategic Contacts Lists in step 2 of the Launch Your Career workbook, or use the online version located at **careerlaunch .academy/resources**.

Specifically, your task is to identify twenty-five professionals to whom you can reach out for career conversations, and to obtain their contact information. Many students like to start with five of their top ten organizations and find five professionals at each one, giving them a total of twenty-five contacts. Students considering smaller organizations or specific roles, such as research assistant, may need to use more than five organizations to get to twenty-five contacts.

> *It takes as much energy to wish as it does to plan.*
>
> —ELEANOR ROOSEVELT

KEY TAKEAWAY #1: HOW TO LEVEL THE PLAYING FIELD

It's possible that some organizations on your top ten list will have online job postings that match your interests, while others won't. Remember that approximately 80% of available jobs are not posted online. It's also possible that you need *any* job, as soon as possible, because of your financial situation and are applying to positions online that are not on your top ten list. Let's examine three scenarios that will reveal how career conversations are the great equalizer for students without connections. Creating relationships with professionals at your desired employers is the key to leveling the playing field. This is sometimes referred to as building social capital.

1. Organizations on Your Top Ten List
That Do Not Have Online Postings

If organizations on your top ten list do not have online postings that are visible to you, don't be discouraged. You can earn a position despite the lack of visible roles, just like Lydia, Marieli, and I did.

Did you know that most of the time, internships and jobs listed on your school's online job portal are shown only to students at certain schools or with specific majors or programs of study? The online job portals used by most colleges and universities are not democratized. Same thing for most of the internet's popular job posting websites. In most instances, employers are given the opportunity to discriminate based on information such as college, major, and job title so that they only show their internships and jobs to candidates with certain criteria. This doesn't provide equal opportunity and it is not fair, but it is not illegal either. All organizations have limited resources, and they often choose to spend those resources on attracting candidates with the characteristics that they think will produce high-quality hires.

Although it makes life easier for employers to focus their hiring efforts only on select schools, majors, or programs of study, you can overcome this obstacle and prove to employers that you are worth recruiting. Many employers will hire students because of their proactive networking efforts—assuming the candidates have the competencies for the internship or job.

One of my students, Juan, wanted to earn a position at a prestigious financial management company, but none recruited at his school and a couple didn't even post their entry-level openings on their own websites. These companies targeted only the most highly ranked schools. The only way for Juan to break into the interviewing process was through proactive outreach. He utilized the Career Launch Method to set up career conversations with people at his desired companies, and these contacts eventually referred him to a hiring manager. He was then invited to join the traditional hiring process and got the job.

Over the past ten years, I've lost count of how many times a student has told me how, just as in Juan's case, an internship or job was made available or created for them because of their strategic and proactive relationship building with professionals.

When approaching organizations that don't have internships or jobs posted online, the best way to get your foot in the door is to find professionals with whom to network. This is especially true at smaller organizations, where mostly senior-level employees make hiring decisions. At larger organizations, networking with midlevel managers often can be the difference maker. In the next few chapters, I will describe how to land a career conversation and turn it into a formal job interview, but for now we'll just focus on finding professionals with whom you can speak.

2. Organizations on Your Top Ten List That Do Have Online Postings

You likely will also apply to organizations with visible job postings. You might be wondering whether you are allowed to both apply online and network to find an internal advocate at the same time. The definitive answer is yes! Often, applying online is an important and necessary step in landing posted roles. Note: In scenarios that are not time sensitive, you may want to strategically use career conversations to develop an internal advocate before submitting the online application. At some organizations, candidates who are referred internally by employees are treated differently than candidates who apply online. If the job posting is time sensitive, you may need to apply online first and simultaneously be working to contact professionals in the department or division where you are applying in an effort to get formal or informal support from current employees. This will set you apart from other candidates who only apply online.

Lots of organizations have an indicator in their hiring software that keeps track of whether the candidate has received referrals from current employees. At organizations without such software, professionals you speak with might directly advocate for you to get the role and pass along your résumé.

Many online job postings receive hundreds, if not thousands, of applications. When a person from human resources does look at your résumé, they are likely to spend only seven seconds skimming it.[1] Except at very small organizations, it is unlikely that the employees to whom you are reaching out will know that you submitted your résumé online. And even if they do know, that is a good thing! You are demonstrating that you are not average. You are the type of person that takes initiative to go above and beyond.

3. Organizations Not on Your Top Ten List That Do Have Online Postings

Perhaps you are committed to pursuing your top ten organizations but you need a job right now—any job, with any organization that will help with your finances, as soon as possible. Create a new list of companies and organizations that have job openings currently available. In addition to submitting your online application, you'll want to do strategic research about who can be helpful to your efforts, so that you can network to find an internal advocate.

What do these three scenarios tell you? Conducting career conversations is key to separating yourself from the competition. Creating a relationship with the hiring manager or employees on the team you could be working with is a great way to differentiate yourself. This is how you level the playing field and give yourself a better chance for success.

A vision without a strategy remains an illusion.

—LEE BOLMAN

STEP 1 **2** 3 4 5 6 7 8

KEY TAKEAWAY #2: IDENTIFY POTENTIAL INTERNAL ADVOCATES

Some employees at your top ten organizations have the ability to be more helpful than others. During your research, you can raise your odds of getting a positive response by being strategic with which employees you choose to contact. Here are four criteria to check when researching employees.

1. Job Function

A job function describes a general category of job roles at an organization, such as finance, nurse, human resources, teacher, marketing, office assistant, design, and so on. Targeting professionals in the job function you are most interested in is a great way to discover insights about your job type of interest. You often can find a professional's job function on their LinkedIn profile or organization's website. If possible, try to find job descriptions for the roles that interest you, to get a better idea about the daily responsibilities of that role.

It's likely that several different job functions may look interesting to you. Conducting career conversations with employees in different departments can be a great way to discover which types of roles would best suit you.

2. Job Title

Hiring managers are employees who are managers or supervisors of other employees. Their titles will be Director of Operations, General Manager, Supervisor, Director of Finance, Senior Manager of Marketing, Senior Director of Sales, Vice President, or similar. These employees are more likely to make hiring decisions than are lower-level employees.

Recruiters are people whose job is to fill job openings. Some recruiters work internally in an organization's human resources department, and others work externally for a different company. Unless you are trying to get a job in human resources or as a recruiter, *do not* target recruiters or human resources using the Career Launch Method. They are likely to direct you to the organization's existing hiring process and are less likely to say yes to a career conversation. You want to prioritize the hiring managers in the departments or divisions of interest. Then, look for nonmanagers.

3. Location
Identify people who are located in an office or work site where you have an interest in working. This is not important if you are looking for a remote position.

4. Shared Interests or Background
When you are searching, it's especially valuable (but not necessary) to identify professionals who share something in common with your interests or background. For example, alumni of your school are more likely to agree to your career conversation requests because they will remember what it was like to be in your position as a student at their alma mater. If you are a community college student, professionals with community college experience from any community college—not just yours—are great people to reach out to. The same logic applies to students pursuing graduate degrees.

Other examples of shared interests and background could include a shared ethnic heritage; a shared international background; a shared hobby (if the professional discusses it on their LinkedIn, personal website, or organization's biography page); or a shared involvement with a sport, community group, foundation, or nonprofit.

HOW TO CONDUCT YOUR RESEARCH

The internet has a range of tools that allow you to efficiently conduct research, find work email addresses, and phone numbers. Start by looking at an organization's website, which sometimes will contain employee biographies. Some organizations include information about current projects or open positions. An organization's social media pages may share relevant links or feature certain employees and their work. Try to find a broad set of employees for each organization. Hiring managers are ideal, but you might also include some entry-level employees currently working in roles you would like to have. Next, use LinkedIn's search and filter tools to find professionals in your desired job functions. Visit **www.careerlaunch.academy/resources** if you are unfamiliar with LinkedIn.

Once you have your list of twenty-five strategic contacts, use an online tool to find their email addresses. Visit **www.careerlaunch.academy/resources** for specific resources and instructions. Or do an online search for "find emails" and you should be able to locate several different sites that allow you to enter in an organization and see the likely format of their email addresses.

Be sure to stay organized as you are researching, to keep track of each employee from each organization and their contact info. I recommend you use the *Launch Your Career Workbook* or a simple spreadsheet. Once you discover a working email for one employee at an organization, you can likely apply that email format to other employees at the organization. Write down as much information about the organizations and employees as possible, including names, job titles, commonalities, and the organization's main phone number, to give yourself more to work with as you begin the next steps of the Career Launch Method.

REVIEW AND REFLECT

- Look online to discover whether there are relevant postings of job openings at the organizations on your top ten list. If there are positions open, you should both apply online and conduct career conversations to meet employees and potentially get a referral. If the organization does not have job postings online, career conversations are even more important and can open new opportunities.

- Your goal in researching employees is to identify potential internal advocates at the organizations where you want to work. Ideally, these employees will work in a job function that interests you, be managers or supervisors, and be working in your desired office location. Also take note of employees who share a common interest or background with you.

- There are many online tools that can help you find the contact information of employees. Start by looking on the organization's website or the person's LinkedIn profile. Then visit **www.careerlaunch.academy/resources** to discover other helpful tools.

ACTION ITEMS

1. Beginning with five of your top ten organizations, strategically identify twenty-five professionals to whom you can reach out for a career conversation.

2. As you research, write down employees' names, job titles, emails, phone numbers (if applicable), and any notes about who they are.

Personal Brand—Enhance Your Online Reputation

Personal brand is the art of becoming knowable, likable, and trustable.

—JOHN JANTSCH

As a rising senior in college, Gavin wanted to put himself in a great position to land a full-time job after graduation. He studied in his university's business program, but there wasn't one specific job title or industry to which he felt especially called. He worried that because his interests and experiences were so varied, companies wouldn't understand what skills he had to offer.

In short, Gavin needed to create an effective and cohesive personal brand.

He started by taking stock of the projects and internships he had recently completed. During his four years of college, Gavin had edited videos for an on-campus organization, interned for a data center company, started a podcast interviewing people at his university, written for the school newspaper, and completed a research project in India. He knew that employers would value the critical thinking and communication skills he had built, but he needed to effectively convey the value he could provide.

Through his research, Gavin discovered that many of the people he admired frequently showed their work online. He decided to create a personal website showcasing the projects he had worked on, both in and out of school.

Gavin discovered that the best portfolios don't just show the final products of a project; they show the *process* of creating that result. Using photos, screenshots, and stories from his past experiences, Gavin created a simple portfolio website. Although he still didn't have great clarity about his future career, Gavin's site showed that he thought deeply about problems, cared about the final products of his work, and could communicate his ideas effectively. The site included a Work page, with links to his projects; an About page, which shared some of Gavin's story; and a Blog page, which included some of the articles he had written for the newspaper.

As senior year began, Gavin decided to begin his job search by targeting management consulting companies. He thought he would enjoy the ability to quickly learn about a variety of industries and to apply his communication and presentation skills to different challenges that companies faced.

With this goal in mind, Gavin moved on to updating his LinkedIn profile, editing his résumé, and writing a cover letter. He wanted to make sure that the skills and experiences he highlighted were consistent across his website, LinkedIn profile, and application materials. He asked several mentors to review his

STEP   1 | 2 | **3** | 4 | 5 | 6 | 7 | 8

résumé and cover letter. Gavin also included a link to his website in his LinkedIn profile, résumé, and email signature.

Gavin's online brand helped him to stand out in a competitive application pool and eventually land a job at the prestigious consulting firm Bain & Company, making him one of the first students from his school that the company had ever hired.

Gavin's experience demonstrates the potential of a strong personal brand. The term "personal brand" refers to how people perceive you based on your skills, your experience, how you treat people, and other information about you. More specifically, your online brand is comprised of the story you tell about yourself online, through your application materials, social media, and any other online mentions of you and your work.

> *What makes you different or weird, that's your strength.*
>
> —MERYL STREEP

Your online brand is essentially the story you present about yourself online, and it is a key step to address before jumping into career conversations, because it helps to build trust when connecting with people you've never met. When you reach out to someone and ask to speak with them, they will naturally want to know who you are. Their first step likely will be to look you up online to ensure that you are a real and genuine person. Even when you are contacting people you already know, these professionals are likely to look at your LinkedIn profile or website to familiarize themselves with you.

If you follow the process laid out in this section, these professionals will be able to easily learn more about you and your work. This will improve your odds of getting a response from your outreach and will build the foundation for a successful career conversation.

Don't think that you need to perfect every detail of your online brand before moving on to step 4. Similar to my advice in step 1, don't overanalyze. The action items in this chapter can be completed quickly and will put you in a great position to begin your outreach.

You may feel like you don't have much to share about yourself and your experiences. You might feel anxious at publishing things online, or frustrated that you haven't done enough of what you want to be doing. Notice these feelings, but give yourself some grace and compassion. Where you are right now is where you will start your journey. Your goal is to create an online brand that feels representative of not just who you are now but also who you want to become.

And remember: You shouldn't have to go on this journey alone. Speaking with your career counselors, professors, or professional mentors can be a great starting place for learning how others view you and deciding what story you want to tell through your personal brand.

> *Your brand is what people say about you when you are not in the room.*
>
> —JEFF BEZOS

KEY TAKEAWAY #1: KNOW YOUR VALUES, GOALS, AND AUDIENCE

You've already completed the first step in personal branding: reflecting on your values, story, and vocation, which you did in step 1. These insights will come in handy for this section and will inform what you choose to communicate about yourself.

Consider your strengths and skills—both your competencies, such as collaboration, adaptability, communication, and leadership, as well as any technical skills you have, such as knowledge of software programs, coding, research analytics, writing, a specialty in the arts, data analysis, or design.

What value can you add to an organization? What type of work do you create? Your online brand—including social media, any type of portfolio, and your application materials—can help answer these questions.

Next, you should think about your goals and the type of opportunities you are seeking. The best practices around personal branding vary quite a bit among different industries. For example, if you are pursuing a position in a creative field like performing arts, graphic design. or software engineering, you should definitely be sharing your work online. If you are interested in a research position, then your online brand should feature your research projects. If you are interested in writing, you should publish examples of your writing online. For most business roles, your LinkedIn profile is the most important aspect of your online brand. And creating an online brand is less essential (but can still be useful) for service-based roles such as teaching, customer service, administrative support, or medicine.

Your goals and desired industry will lead you to reflect on your audience of potential employers and what they value. For most students, the audience for your online brand will be professionals and recruiters in the industry or industries in which you are interested. Which of your strengths would a hiring manager find valuable? What accomplishments and experiences would people in your desired industry value? Thinking through each of these questions will help you decide which information to share about yourself and what themes of content you may want to share online.

Let me share a few final thoughts on how to think about your personal brand. First, it's completely fine if you are considering multiple types of work and have diverse interests. You don't need to pigeonhole yourself into one career field; even having a general idea of your audience will be helpful in completing the actions in the next section.

Second, your personal brand should strike a balance between authenticity and professionalism. On one hand, you should try to be as authentic as possible, because people will appreciate your humanity and personality. However, you shouldn't share anything you would be uncomfortable with a supervisor seeing. This is a personal decision, and you can choose how much information you want to share online. With everything you share about yourself, of course, you want to put your best foot forward to position yourself to land an internship or job.

> *Start by knowing what you want and who you are, build credibility around it, and deliver it online in a compelling way.*
>
> —KRISTA NEHER

KEY TAKEAWAY #2: CREATE YOUR EMAIL SIGNATURE, LINKEDIN PROFILE, AND PORTFOLIO

Entire books have been written about personal branding, but in this section, I'm going to focus on three simple actions you can take that will set you apart from the competition and communicate your value to professionals: an email signature, a LinkedIn profile, and a portfolio. **Creating an email signature is essential before beginning outreach, as is creating a basic LinkedIn profile. But it isn't necessary to build a more advanced LinkedIn profile or to make a portfolio before beginning step 4.**

STEP | 1 | 2 | **3** | 4 | 5 | 6 | 7 | 8 |

1. Email Signature

To maximize your success during your outreach efforts, you need to create a professional email signature for your school email account. You can also do the same for your personal email. Providing your audience with relevant information about you is an important way to bolster your credibility and to get professionals to say yes to your outreach for career conversations.

At the very least, include your name, a head shot photo, major or program of study, school, and a link to your LinkedIn profile. (We'll cover LinkedIn next.) Including a head shot in your email signature can make the professional you're emailing more comfortable by providing a face to go with your name. For

Henry Gabriel

Penn State, Sociology
VP of Multicultural Center
(123) 456-7890
www.linkedin.com/in/henrygabriel123

Sonia Gonzalez

Medial Assistant Program
San Diego City College
(123) 456-7890
www.linkedin.com/in/sonia-p-gonzalez

Nancy Norfolk

Art & Design Intern, Games Media Co.
University of Iowa
LinkedIn: www.linkedin.com/in/nancynorfolk
(123) 456-7890

FIGURE 2. *Email signatures.*

consistency, it's best practice to use the same head shot in your email signature and your LinkedIn profile. Enabling professionals to learn more about you by clicking on your LinkedIn link after receiving your emails is an easy way to increase your odds of getting a response to your outreach requests.

I have more than ten years of student data that suggests that you need these elements in your email signature to optimize your chances of a professional agreeing to meet with you. For more information on how to create an email signature, or to use one of our templates, visit **www.careerlaunch.academy/resources**. Figure 2 presents several examples of excellent email signatures. Some information is kept confidential here, but you get the idea.

2. LinkedIn Profile

Most professionals who receive a message from you will look you up before responding. If you are reaching out in a professional context, they will most likely look at your LinkedIn profile. LinkedIn is the world's biggest professional network, with more than 722 million users all over the world in 2021. This professional networking website has more than 20 million job postings and pages for 50 million companies.[1] Creating a complete LinkedIn profile will help showcase your experience and skills to future employers and to the professionals you contact for career conversations, making you more trustworthy and credible.

If you have followed the first step of creating an email signature that includes your LinkedIn URL, you make it especially easy for anyone you email to learn more about you. Here are a few tips to strengthen your LinkedIn profile:

Add a professional profile photo. A high-quality profile photo makes your profile more credible, unique, and authentic. It doesn't have to be a professional photo. A picture from a camera

phone is fine. Try to get a picture where your head takes up about half the frame. Your profile photo should be well lit and have a relatively simple background.

Edit your headline. A headline is automatically created based on your current position, but you may want to edit your headline. A generic headline like "Student at XYZ College" is okay, but you may want to include multiple phrases separated by the vertical dash character, like this: "Administrative Assistant at Local Art Gallery | History Major at XYZ College | Aspiring Teacher." Try to think about what high-level overview of you would be both accurate and eye-catching.

About

I am a 2nd year student at De Anza College studying business administration. A year ago, I spoke with an Portfolio Manager at BlackRock about the power of passive investment through ETFs, which sparked my interest in portfolio management.

In my first two years at De Anza College, I have furthered my understanding of business and investments through classwork and business simulations. I improve operations at De Anza College's help desk by providing positive customer support.

I am currently looking for an internship in portfolio management. If you have a position opening or would like to talk about business, you can reach me at john.smith@example.com

---

FIGURE 3. *An effective LinkedIn "About" section.*

Add a summary. This overview of yourself should be at least one paragraph but no more than three paragraphs in length. You can tell a short backstory about what you are interested in and why. This section is a great place to show some of your personality, too.

The final paragraph can say what you are currently looking for, such as "I am currently looking for a summer internship in health care. If you know of an open position or would like to chat about _____, email me at _____."

Finance/Treasury Intern
Medical System
May 2020 – Sep 2020 · 5 mos
Sacramento, California, United States

- Automated parts of exposure forecast by creating a predictive Excel model
- Analyzed forecast information to identify major changes in 4 currencies' exposure
- Designed diagrams and data visualizations to communicate cash flow trends
- Created current event reports on currency rates and market conditions

Digital Marketing Coordinator
Blue Nebraska
Apr 2019 – Nov 2019 · 8 mos
Omaha, Nebraska, United States

I contributed to 3 out of the 5 marketing units for the healthcare company Blue Nebraska. My responsibilities included strategic planning for new marketing initiatives, managing social media accounts, creating infographics, and supervising an event-planning intern.

I also worked closely with the Digital Marketing Manager, assisting with campaigns for member engagement and generating leads for B2B outreach. After three months on the job, I was promoted from Marketing Associate to Digital Marketing Coordinator.

FIGURE 4. *LinkedIn "Experience" sections.*

Work experience. Like your résumé, your LinkedIn profile should highlight your relevant jobs, internships, and volunteer experiences. Fill out each section of the Work Experience form on your LinkedIn profile. In the description section, explain how you have added value to that organization. Make sure you're highlighting your biggest accomplishments, using quantitative measurements when possible. Figure 4 shows two examples, one using bullet points, as in a résumé, and the other using a paragraph-style description.

Education. Fill out the education section on LinkedIn and include any relevant details that could differentiate you, such as a high GPA, leadership in a student organization, participation in athletics or performing arts, or any honors or awards. If your GPA is below 3.5, do not include it, since it likely won't set you apart.

In addition, there are some advanced LinkedIn tips that you may wish to employ. Visit **www.careerlaunch.academy/ resources** to find short tutorials on the suggestions given here.

Custom URL. Creating a custom URL based on your name can make it easy for recruiters and hiring managers to find you. Ideally, your custom URL should be the same as your name, perhaps with a dash or underscore in the middle or a number at the end if necessary, such as www.linkedin.com/in/jane-doe. Be sure to add your custom LinkedIn URL to your résumé, in addition to your email signature.

Add media. If there are any websites or articles that show the work you've done, or reference an accomplishment, you can link the website or upload an image or PDF.

Ask for a recommendation. If you don't already have a LinkedIn recommendation or two, consider contacting a former supervisor, coach, or professor to ask them for a recommendation. This greatly enhances your credibility. But do not use LinkedIn's built-in function to initially ask for a recommendation. This is an important request and it's relationship-oriented so you should first ask on the phone, via video chat, or in person. Once you receive a verbal confirmation, then send the request via LinkedIn.

If you have a letter of recommendation on paper but not on LinkedIn, I suggest that you ask the recommender to add their recommendation on LinkedIn. Some professionals may not have a LinkedIn account. If that is the case, you might upload a letter of recommendation on LinkedIn using the "Add Media" option.

Regardless of the format of your recommendation, however, it can be a valuable tool in your job search as a source of credibility.

3. Portfolio

Creating a portfolio will differentiate you and can provide a competitive advantage over other students when applying to any job or contacting any professional. In the story at the beginning of this chapter, Gavin created his portfolio on a personal website. There are many free website builders that allow you to create a simple website without coding. This will require a time investment up front to get the design and content just like you want it, but it can pay dividends down the line.

However, there are simpler ways to create a portfolio. Check with your school to see if it has an online portfolio tool for you to use. Another simple option is to create a Google Slides presentation. You can create a portfolio using this method, regardless of whether you have ever had an internship or formal work experience. Class projects and volunteer experiences will work just fine. If you have worked in a job you feel is unrelated to your career goals (such as fast food, yard work, or retail), you still can use these experiences in a portfolio. *Which* experiences you show matters less than the *skills* you display and the *process* of your thinking.

Here's how to make a Google Slides portfolio: If you have a nonschool Google account, create your portfolio from there so that you can create a public link (set the sharing settings to "anyone with the link can view"). If you use your school Google account, you may need to download the presentation as a PDF and then email it because your school may have sharing restrictions.

Begin building the presentation based on your goals, values, and résumé. Include one or two introduction slides with your photo and a brief explanation of who you are, what you study, and what you are interested in. Next, create several slides for each project or experience you want to highlight. For each experience, give some context about the situation, the organization, and the challenge you helped to solve. Talk about your work process and your contribution to the project. If you have images or videos that show your work or make the slideshow visually interesting, be sure to include them.

Make sure to send your portfolio to several professional mentors to edit—you want your portfolio to be polished and visually pleasing. Once you finish, you can hyperlink the presentation in your email signature (if using a nonschool account) or send a PDF version along with your résumé when applying for a job.

REVIEW AND REFLECT

- Your online personal brand is the story that your online presence communicates to people who don't know you. Think about what story you want to share with professionals and employers.

- Remember that you don't need to be an expert in anything; it can be just as powerful to show your process and interests.

- The most essential elements of your personal brand to continue forward in the Career Launch Method are a professional email signature and a basic LinkedIn profile. When you have time, build a more advanced LinkedIn profile and create a portfolio, but don't let these steps prevent you from moving forward to step 4.

ACTION ITEMS

1. Think about the following questions, which will inform your personal brand: What skills do you want to display? What experiences would employers find valuable? How can you communicate these skills and experiences in your online brand?

2. Create an email signature with your name, photo, school, major or program of study, and LinkedIn profile link.

3. Spend time working on your LinkedIn profile. Make sure you have completed all the basics (photo, headline, and education). Then consider more advanced ways to highlight yourself—for example, by adding media to the work experience section or asking professionals to write you a recommendation.

4. If you are actively applying for internships or jobs, make sure that your résumé and cover letter effectively communicate your personal brand story. Gain feedback from résumé software your career center may provide, as well as your professors, career counselors/coaches, or mentors to help you best present yourself.

5. When you have time, create a portfolio using Google Slides, your school's portfolio tool (if available), or if you, or if you want, a personal website. Showcase your interests, skills, and experiences, then get feedback from others. Link this portfolio to your email signature, download it as a PDF to send with your résumé, and/or use it in job applications.

Outreach—How to Play the Student Card to Set Up Career Conversations

Strategy without tactics is the slowest route to victory. Tactics without strategy is the noise before defeat.

—SUN TZU

Ever since Kevin could remember, his parents had told him that if he worked hard, he could achieve anything. Kevin's parents operate a small doughnut shop, working seven days per week for most of the year. Their dedication is what made it possible for Kevin to go to college and pursue a career he'd love. After two years of community college, Kevin transferred to a four-year university. He chose finance as a major but didn't have a great idea of what he wanted to do for a career. Although he performed well in school, Kevin wasn't able to land the internships he really wanted. Kevin thought that the sports business industry might match his interests, but he had no connections with anyone in that field who might help him get started.

During his junior year, Kevin took my class, and he used the strategies and tactics to try to land an internship. Kevin, an introvert with a pronounced stutter at times, had never done outreach like this before, so he was pretty nervous and doubted the strategy's effectiveness for someone like him. During his research, Kevin was searching online and found Don Yee, the agent for MVP quarterback Tom Brady. He added Mr. Yee to his list of twenty-five contacts.

Yee was very successful and no doubt very busy, so Kevin assumed that he wouldn't have time to meet with a student like him. Nevertheless, Kevin followed the outreach strategy detailed in this chapter. He sent an initial email to Yee and then, when he didn't get a response, sent a follow-up email two business days later. A couple days after that, he worked up the courage to call the main office phone number. No one answered, so he left a message, but he didn't think anything more would come of this shot in the dark.

To his surprise, Yee's assistant returned Kevin's call a few hours later. On the voicemail, Kevin had explained his situation as a student and what he hoped to learn from Yee. He asked for twenty minutes of Yee's time to get career advice. The assistant received approval from Yee and offered either a video chat or an in-person meeting. Kevin told her that he wanted to meet in person, even though it required a six-hour drive.

During the meeting, Yee was impressed that Kevin had made such a great effort to travel to his office. Kevin's twenty-minute meeting ended up lasting for more than two hours. Yee walked him through his whole career path and gave Kevin valuable advice about how to break into the sports industry. He took note of Kevin's curiosity and willingness to learn. At the end of the meeting, Yee told Kevin that he had an opening at his agency and asked whether he would like to join as a paid intern. This was Kevin's dream internship, so he accepted with great delight, and worked at the agency Yee & Dubin for the summer.

This experience showed Kevin just how helpful professionals can be, so he continued to be proactive about meeting professionals during his internship. He connected with as many people at the firm as he could, building a solid base of connections in the sports management industry. Although Kevin mostly enjoyed the work, he wasn't altogether sure if it was right for him. One of his mentors at the company gave him a truthful perspective on the upsides and downsides of the industry, and Kevin eventually realized in his discernment process that being a sports agent wasn't right for him.

Although Kevin's dream internship didn't turn into a long-term career, it was still an important learning experience and a turning point in gaining the self-confidence to pursue careers he was passionate about. He also practiced valuable skills that have benefited him in the years since the internship. After the summer internship ended, Kevin continued to conduct career conversations during his senior year. He later decided to attend graduate school and transitioned to his career of choice in data analytics.

Kevin's story demonstrates that conducting career conversations can help you overcome self-doubt and achieve things you didn't know were possible. His authenticity and curiosity were apparent to everyone with whom he spoke, and this led to many of these people becoming long-term connections, who to this day continue to offer him valuable advice. Kevin is also a great example of why I advise students to follow the ten-day outreach strategy discussed in this chapter. Well-timed and polite follow-up messages are key to getting professionals to say yes to meeting with you. Don Yee shared with Kevin that he doesn't respond to student requests via email or LinkedIn, but he admires students willing to reach out with a phone call.

"Not every connection will lead to a long-lasting relationship," Kevin said. "But some career conversations will lead to strong connections, and you can maintain those relationships throughout your career. The Career Launch Method changed my life and provided opportunities I previously thought were impossible to obtain. Learning how to effectively build relationships with professionals has given me an unshakable self-confidence, which I believe is the main reason my stutter has gone away."

> *You have to take advantage of the opportunity of a lifetime, in the lifetime of the opportunity.*
>
> —ERIC THOMAS

KEY TAKEAWAY #1: PLAY THE STUDENT CARD

Many students feel that *because* they are a student, no one who is further along or established in their career will want to speak with them. Students often have the false idea that they have nothing to contribute to such a conversation and that they would just be wasting people's time. But in fact your status as a student doesn't hurt you; it actually *helps* you to build relationships with professionals. As chapter 4 pointed out, professionals remember what it was like to be a student with little or no work experience and few connections. Many people take joy in paying it forward by meeting with students to discern their future and by opening doors to internships and jobs and/or by making introductions to other professionals. When you follow the Career Launch Method, you will be reaching out to professionals in a respectful manner and expressing gratitude for the time they spend meeting you, which will make professionals more likely to want to help you.

Playing the "student card" means that when you do outreach, you intentionally say that you are a student who is looking to learn.

My recommendation is that you go one step beyond mentioning that you are a student by stating that you have an assignment to conduct career conversations. This greatly increases your chances of professionals wanting to help you. Each term, I give my students an assignment to complete at least two career conversations, and I'd like to extend this "assignment" to you as well. I'm giving you this assignment because I want you to ethically use the student card when you reach out to professionals using the templates on the following pages. I may not teach at the school you attend, but that doesn't mean I can't give you this important assignment. Of course, there will be nothing to turn in—unless you are reading or listening to this book for a class taught by another professor who gives you a similar assignment.

Students often wonder what happens when they graduate. If you're a recent graduate, it doesn't make sense to say you have a class assignment, but you can still play the "recent graduate card." It's an extremely common experience (especially in the wake of the COVID-19 pandemic) for new graduates to be going through a period of vocational discernment and job searching. Professionals like to help recent graduates for the same reasons that they like to help students. The Career Launch Method even works well for professionals in their late twenties and thirties. I've had many former students reach out and tell me they played the "young professional card." In their outreach, they state that they are a young professional looking to learn and build their career.

> *Knowledge is not power. Knowledge is potential power. Action is power.*
>
> —TONY ROBBINS

KEY TAKEAWAY #2: USE PROVEN OUTREACH STRATEGIES AND TEMPLATES

The two main types of outreach that you need to learn about are cold networking and warm networking. Cold networking involves contacting someone without having any previous relationship with that person. Warm networking involves making use of your personal network, such as family, friends, neighbors, career counselors, professors, former coaches, and teachers, as well as alumni platforms, if your college has one.

Many students initially think they don't know anyone who could help them make introductions through warm networking, but you should spend a good amount of time brainstorming before you move on to cold networking. Think about family friends, former coaches or mentors, people in the groups to which you belong, high school teachers, and so on. It's okay if you haven't spoken to a particular person in a while. Many of these people likely will be willing to help you if you ask. The key is to connect with as many of these people as you can—even if they don't have the career you're interested in. Some of the people, unbeknownst to you, might know others who *do* have careers you're considering, and they can make introductions for you.

Some students are fortunate to have many people with whom they can do meaningful warm networking that can lead to several career conversations. But the majority of students do not come from families, colleges, or circumstances that provide connections

STEP 1 | 2 | 3 | **4** | 5 | 6 | 7 | 8

to people with access to the internships, jobs, or organizations in which they are interested. In this case, which was my situation, you need to engage primarily in cold networking.

Many students think warm networking is superior to cold networking because it relies on existing connections. Although requests made through existing connections may have a higher success rate, my research with Barry Posner has found that *students who engage in cold networking are twice as likely to earn an internship than students who engage only in warm networking.* It is uncommon for students to already know the right professionals at organizations where they're applying, so cold and warm networking is almost always required to connect with the right people for your interests.

The idea of reaching out to complete strangers isn't very appealing to most students. But by taking the actions and utilizing the templates detailed here, you can equip yourself and be more confident in reaching out to professionals who can be beneficial to your career.

Strategies and Templates for Warm Networking

Three main groups of people can be beneficial in warm networking. If your college has an alumni platform, that will be an additional resource. I've provided some templates on how to contact people from each group. **Remember that you should always customize a template so that it's specific to the person you are contacting.** No one likes to feel like they are receiving a copy-and-paste message. However, these templates do include the key information that you should include in your outreach messages. They are useful in setting up a conversation with one of your existing connections who has a career in which you might be interested, or who may know other people to whom you could be introduced. If you have a strong relationship with someone,

you may feel comfortable just asking them directly for connections or for someone's contact information via text message. Most of the time, though, it's respectful and wise to have a conversation with your connection (verbally or via email) to give them more background on your career ambitions and the type of professionals with whom you want to connect. Here are templates for three common types of warm connections.

1. For people you know and feel comfortable contacting

Hi, [Name],

I have an assignment this [semester/quarter/summer] to conduct two career conversations. Can we schedule 15–20 minutes to connect later this week or next week?

Thank you,
[Your Name]

2. For people you know but haven't talked to in a while and are unsure if you can or should reach out to them

Hi, [Name],

It's been a while, and I hope you are doing well. This is [Your Name] from [how you know them]. I have an assignment this [semester/quarter/summer] to conduct two career conversations. Can we schedule 15–20 minutes to connect later this week or next week?

Thank you for your consideration,
[Your Name]

3. **For people that your professors, friends, counselors, classmates, or family know but whom you don't know personally, or for people on an alumni platform**

If you want to be introduced to a specific person

Hi, [Name],

I hope you are doing well. [personalize as needed but don't be too lenghty]

I have an assignment this [semester/quarter/summer] about career discernment. You are connected with [Name of Person you want to connect to] and I'd be most appreciative if you could introduce me and/or provide me with [his/her] email address. I would like to connect with [her/him] for my assignment.

Thank you,
[Your Name]

If you want help finding people in a certain industries or job types

Hi, [Name],

I hope you are doing well.

I have an assignment this [semester/quarter/summer] about career discernment. I would love to speak with people in [industry name(s) and job type(s)] or who work for [Organization Name(s)].

I'm interested in learning more about [job function] and was wondering if you know anyone who might be helpful in this assignment. If you are comfortable sending an introductory email or sending me their contact information, I would really appreciate it.

Thank you,
[Your Name]

Strategies and Templates for Cold Networking

Cold networking will always be more challenging than warm networking, which is why I advocate starting with warm networking. As you begin your cold networking, keep in mind that alumni of your college and people with similarities to you are more likely to respond to your requests. However, if you completed the action items in step 3 and you demonstrate professional persistence by following each of the steps in the outreach strategy given here, you will be surprised how many people will respond positively to your messages—even professionals who aren't alumni or who aren't similar to you.

In the templates that follow, you are explicitly asking for an in-person or video chat meeting. In our research, Barry Posner and I found that, compared with phone calls, in-person or video meetings double the odds of career conversations leading to employment opportunities. In-person meetings are ideal, but they aren't always feasible, so video chats are second best. Because the other person can see you and your facial expressions, they will feel like they know you better than if they can't see your face. Phone calls are far from ideal but will suffice if they are the only option.

TEN-DAY OUTREACH STRATEGY

Let me note a few important distinctions. First, starting your outreach with a LinkedIn note does not optimize success. Second, do not give up after sending one email. Over the past ten-plus years, I've taught a variety of outreach strategies. Some have worked and some haven't. The strategy below is what has proven to be optimal. It may not be the quickest method, but it gives you the best chance to get a yes. Third, do not reach out to more than five professionals at a time. Although it might be tempting, trust me on this one. I've had students disregard this advice and then admit that they became disorganized or overwhelmed and made mistakes that cost them opportunities.

Starting with LinkedIn is a common shortcut that students want to take. While LinkedIn is an excellent resource, it should not be your first mode of outreach. This doesn't mean it's impossible to get a yes by starting with LinkedIn; it just means LinkedIn messages don't maximize your chances.

Do not give up after sending your initial outreach. Follow-up is extremely important for getting professionals to say yes, i.e. Kevin's experience with Don Yee. Many students are apprehensive about following up after their initial outreach because they feel that they will be perceived as pushy or aggressive. However, the main reason that you don't hear back from your inquiries is that professionals are just busy and will ignore your request unless you follow up with another message. Some professionals have told me that they purposely don't respond to initial cold outreach to "see if the student really wants it."

Keep in mind that your goal is to be respectful and to get the person you are contacting to give you a yes. Most people will tell you no or will never respond, and that's okay! Don't take it personally. That's why you made a list of twenty-five in step 2. Continued action gets rewarded. Remember, it's a numbers game. You need to persist because although one single conversation is unlikely to change your life, one single conversation *can* change your life.

Day 1: Email #1 to contacts 1 through 5.

Day 3: Email #2 to contacts 1 through 5.

Day 5: Call contacts 1 through 5.

Day 7: LinkedIn message to contacts 1 through 5.

Day 9: Print and mail a letter. If not possible, send email #3 with résumé attached.

Day 10: Stop contacting these five people and repeat the process with five more contacts from your list of twenty-five.

Note: "Days" here includes business days only, not weekends or holidays. If day 1 falls on a Friday, then day 3 would be Tuesday.

> *While one person hesitates because they feel inferior, another is busy making mistakes and becoming superior.*
>
> —HENRY C. LINK

Day 1 Email Template

Sending a clear and concise email is essential to landing a career conversation. The template offered here has been refined based students' experiences. Remember to customize the template in ways that indicate you have done your research and know what your contact does. **All emails should be sent from your school email address, not your personal email. This proves that you are actually a student.**

STEP | 1 | 2 | 3 | **4** | 5 | 6 | 7 | 8 |

For the subject line, I recommend that you use the name of your college, which will make the receiver curious enough to open the email without giving enough information for them to immediately disregard and delete your request. This strategy is called "gating," a concept that considers the intended audience's behavior along the path of their decision-making.

The first objective of your cold email is for the email to not get deleted before it actually gets opened and read. Imagine a busy doctor or business professional who has just finished back-to-back-to-back meetings. When they glance at their phone, they might have twenty-three emails in their inbox. If your subject line says "Informational Interview" or "Coffee Chat" or something similar, your email might get deleted before it gets read. Using the name of your college is purposely vague and your email likely will be opened and reviewed.

> Subject line: [Name of Your College]
>
> Hi, [Name],
>
> I'm a student at [Name of Your College]. I have an assignment this [quarter/semester/summer] to conduct two 20-minute career conversations via video chat or in person with [companies or organizations] and people that interest me.
>
> You've had a successful career since you finished college at [Name of College]. I'd like to learn about your journey from [Name of First Organization after college] to [Name of Current Organization]. (*Optional: add a second sentence and say more about what you want to learn about.*)

I understand you probably keep a busy schedule, so I'm willing to meet before or after business hours, if necessary. Are you available on [Tuesday afternoon or Friday morning]?

I hope it's okay that I'm sending this email, and I look forward to hearing back from you.

Thank you,
[Your Name]
[Your Email Signature]

Note: If the person did not attend college or has worked for the same organization for their entire career, you will need to modifiy accordingly. The body of this email template is very intentional. First, give some thought to the greeting line. A general rule of thumb is to use Mr. or Ms. for professionals, especially for those in their forties and older. For younger professionals, and in some industries and geographies, it may be appropriate to greet professionals by their first name.

Second, you will state that you're a student and you have an assignment to conduct two career conversations via video chat or in person. It's important to explicitly call out the modality, because you don't want a phone call. However, you should remove "in person" for people who aren't located near you or during times of a pandemic.

Next, you pay a compliment and mention a few things that are specific to them as an individual. This shows that you truly researched them and are not just copying and pasting the email.

Then you want to acknowledge that they have a busy schedule and convey your willingness to meet before or after business hours if needed. This sentence is very important, because the number one reason that professionals say no is that they are too busy. There is a communication principle that says the best time to handle an objection is before it comes up. That is what you are doing here. Can someone still tell you that they are too busy? Of course. But it's less likely to occur. Another benefit of the sentence is that it showcases something about your personal brand. You are implying that you are a go-getter, an overachiever who is willing to meet early or late, and that you have empathy for their busy schedule.

Finally, you want to provide two time slots that can work for you. If you have a tight schedule, you may need to offer specific times, as opposed to chunks of time. Even though you are the one making the request, professionals recognize that you have a class schedule and likely a job too, and thus it's best practice for you to proactively provide a couple of time slots that work for you. This minimizes the amount of back-and-forth emails, which saves time and increases your chances of getting a yes. If your proposed time slots don't work for the professional, they will likely offer other options. If you simply state something like "Are you willing to meet with me sometime?," you are less likely to be successful.

Day 3 Email Template

Most professionals won't respond to your initial email, so be prepared to follow up two business days later (remember that weekends don't count). Start a brand-new email, but use the same subject line as your first one. This follow-up email needs to be concise and polite. Here's the template that works best:

> Subject line: [Name of Your College]
>
> Hi, [Name],
>
> I hope your week is going well.
>
> I am thrilled at the possibility of meeting with you for a 20-minute career conversation for my school assignment.

Would [next Wednesday or Friday] work for you?

Thank you,
[Your Name]
[Your Email Signature]

Day 5 Phone Call Template

If neither of your first two emails elicits a response, try a phone call. People in some job types are more likely than others to pick up the phone, but leaving a voice mail is always a good strategy to get a response. I recognize that making a phone call is much more intimidating than sending an email or LinkedIn message. But this is the exact reason that professionals are more likely to say yes to students who do not skip this step. Although making a phone call may induce fear or concern, consider that the worst-case scenario is that you leave a message and stumble over your words, or the person could even pick up and say, "No, I'm too busy to meet." The best case, though, is that your phone call leads to a career conversation, which can lead to an internship or job.

Is it worth letting your fears and concerns prevent you from calling when a "yes" could change your life? Remember Kevin's story from the beginning of the chapter: the phone call made all the difference. There are lots of professionals who will never respond to emails or LinkedIn messages but will say yes to a phone call or voicemail.

Try to find the person's direct work phone number online, though it is unlikely that you will be successful in this. You are probably going to be calling a main line and one of two things will likely happen: Either you will enter an automated phone tree (along the lines of "Press 1 for . . .") or you will speak with a receptionist. If you enter a phone tree, great. Navigate the prompts and leave a voice mail if the person doesn't answer.

STEP | 1 | 2 | 3 | **4** | 5 | 6 | 7 | 8 |

When you are speaking with a receptionist, say, "[First Name, Last Name], please." Notice you aren't saying that you are a student calling for a class assignment. Make it sound like you already know the person. There's a saying in the workplace, "Don't make a request to someone who can tell you no but cannot tell you yes." Receptionists and assistants can tell you no but they can't tell you yes. Do not use the template with a receptionist unless you have to.

Note: Many companies have two main lines, one for customer service and one for the organization's headquarters. You want to locate the latter.

This template gives you an idea of what to say either when leaving a message or when you get the professional you want to speak with on the line.

> Hi, [Their Name]. This is [Your Name]. I'm a student at [Name of College].
>
> (*If the person answers, pause and let them acknowledge you.*)
>
> I have an assignment to conduct two twenty-minute career conversations, on a video chat or in person, with people and organizations that interest me.
>
> I'd like to learn about your journey from [Name of First Organization after college] to [Name of Organization where they are working now] because I'm interested in [name of industry or job function].
>
> I understand you probably keep a busy schedule, so I'm willing to meet before or after business hours, if necessary. Are you available on [time slot] or [time slot]?
>
> (*If you are leaving voice mail, add . . .*) Please call me back at [phone number]. That's [repeat number]. Thank you so much. I look forward to hearing from you.

STEP   1 | 2 | 3 | **4** | 5 | 6 | 7 | 8

Note: Make sure the voice mail box on your phone is set up and is not full. Also, make sure to record a personalize greeting on your voice mail. I've had employers tell me they have called students to say yes to career conversations, and even to offer

FIGURE 5. *Sending a LinkedIn invite.*

STEP 1 2 3 **4** 5 6 7 8

jobs, but couldn't leave a voice mail, so they moved on. You do not want this to happen to you.

Day 7 LinkedIn Message

If professionals don't respond to your emails or phone call (or if you can't find their phone number), LinkedIn is your next mode of outreach. To send someone a connection request that includes a message on LinkedIn, go to their profile and click Connect. It's essential that you add a note (space is limited) to say why you want to connect (see figure 5). *If* you see that the person you are contacting is active on LinkedIn, you might consider doing this step even earlier in the process.

> Hi, [Name],
>
> I'm a student at [Name of College] and I have an assignment to conduct two career conversations via video chat or in person. I'd love to connect for 20 minutes and learn about your career.
>
> I'm willing to talk before or after business hours if necessary.
>
> Thanks,
> [Your Name]

Day 9: Mail a Letter or Email #3 with Résumé Attached

Physical mail is unconventional these days, and that is exactly why it is such an effective strategy. If your contact works in an office and you can find the address, you should mail a typed letter along with your résumé, giving a bit of background on who you are and asking for a career conversation.

Sending a letter is ideal because it's likely to be read. To optimize your chances for success, this tactic requires you to print a letter (asking for a career conversation) and your résumé (ideally on thick card stock paper), to purchase an oversize envelope (9 × 12 inches) so you don't have to fold your letter or résumé, to buy postage, and then to send it off in the mail. Figure 6 presents a template for how to address an envelope to an organization. This takes time, and each mailing costs the price of a latte, but it might be worth it for you, as it was for me.

If mailing isn't an option, send email #3, and make sure to attach your résumé as a PDF. This email should be short and should request that the professional will keep you in mind for any opportunities and/or will forward your résumé on to a coworker.

> Subject line: Keep me in mind—[Your Name], résumé attached
>
> Hi, [Name],
>
> I know you keep a busy schedule, but I hope our paths will cross down the road.
>
> Please keep me in mind for any opportunities and/or forward my attached résumé on to a coworker.
>
> Many thanks,
> [Your Name]
> [Your Email Signature]

At this point in the follow-up process, you don't need to ask for a career conversation. You are better off sending this note and including your résumé. The professional probably won't be able to meet with you, but they might forward your email to a coworker. This doesn't take much effort on their part, and it's worth a shot. One of my former students, Kyle, landed a full-time job in Boston using this approach.

STEP 1 | 2 | 3 | **4** | 5 | 6 | 7 | 8

FIGURE 6. *How to address an envelope.*

If you do not receive a response after executing these five modes of outreach, STOP. Cross the person off your list of twenty-five and move on to the next contact.

HANDLING OBJECTIONS

Sometimes you will get a hard no. *When this happens, you must stop contacting that professional and move on to other people on your list.* You should always be polite and respectful, which means honoring the professional's request in this scenario.

Other times, people will give you some kind of reason or objection to your request. These are called rebuttals. Rebuttals are *not* the same as a no, and you shouldn't give up. Here are three of the most frequent rebuttals and how you should consider responding.

1. "I'm busy."

(*To which you respond . . .*)

Hi, [Name],

No problem. I understand. I am willing to meet with you when your schedule is not so busy. I would really appreciate the opportunity to learn about your career and experiences.

Can we find a time next month? If so, when is best for you?

Also, if there is any chance you can meet sooner, I will be flexible with my schedule.

Thank you for your consideration.
[Your Name]

2. "Yes, but can we do this by phone?"

(*To which you respond . . .*)

Hi, [Name],

Thank you for getting back to me. I am excited and grateful for this opportunity.

I've been instructed to complete these career conversations by video chat or in person. If that is not possible, I am happy to connect by phone. I understand that talking on the phone can be better from a time management perspective. However, I hope you might consider making yourself available for an in-person visit or video call.

If you can accommodate a meeting in person or a video call, I can be flexible with the date and time. If not, I look forward to connecting by phone.

Thank you for your consideration.
[Your Name]

3. "It's not a good time."

(*To which you respond . . .*)

Hi, [Name],

Okay, no problem. I'll make a note to reconnect with you in a month and hopefully it will be a better time for you.

Thank you for your consideration.
[Your Name]

REQUESTS FOR MORE INFORMATION

Other times, people will give you a maybe type of answer. Here are a few common questions you can expect to receive, along with how you should consider responding.

1. "Are you looking for a job?"

(*To which you respond . . .*)

Hi, [Name],

Thanks for asking. What I am looking for is an opportunity to learn about your experience, your background, and your organization. I'd like to know about your own career. If you are looking to hire, I would certainly be interested in knowing about that; however, that is not the reason for my request.

Can we find a time to connect next week?

[Your Name]

Note that we are again using the strategy of gating.

2. "How did you find my email?"

Just be honest. All the resources this book provides are legal and ethical. Tell the person exactly where you found their contact information. You can reference this book. Don't forget to follow up your response to this question with some variation of your prepared script, to see whether this person would be willing to have an in-person or video chat meeting with you!

3. "What questions will you be asking me?"

Go ahead and share a few of the questions that you will develop after reading step 5, and ask if these seem okay or acceptable. Then ask if the person is available sometime the following week. Don't reveal, however, the "Advanced Preparation" questions (which will be discussed in step 6).

BEGIN YOUR OUTREACH

Take some time to review your warm and cold contacts and decide where it makes sense for you to get started. You should first think about your existing network and follow the warm networking strategies. Next, choose five professionals from your list of twenty-five and follow the ten-day outreach strategy for each. You'll be sending a lot of emails, so I recommend using the Outreach Tracking Sheets in the *Launch Your Career Workbook* or the online version located at **careerlaunch.academy/resources** for tracking your requests, who responds, and when you set up career conversations. Remember to persist through each part of the ten-day outreach guide, and keep a positive attitude when someone says no or is slow to respond.

Note: When you receive a "yes" and you finalize a date and time, it is your responsibility to send the professional a calendar invite for the career conversation. You should assume that the person is busy and that they will need a calendar event to remember your meeting. Use your school email calendar to create a new event and invite the other person's email to that event. Reference the *Workbook* to view an example or do a quick online search if you're unfamiliar with sending a calendar invitation.

REVIEW AND REFLECT

- Playing the "student card" means that when you do outreach, you intentionally say that you are a student who is looking to learn. Professionals enjoy helping students and recent graduates.

- Warm networking is when you do outreach to people with whom you have some connection or introduction. These include friends of friends, family connections, professors at school, or people you once knew but have fallen out of touch with. Warm networking is a great place to begin your outreach. Follow the templates in this chapter to get started.

- Cold networking is when you reach out to people whom you have never met. It is likely that you will need to do cold networking to meet people in the job functions at the organizations where you want to work.

- Following the ten-day outreach strategy is essential to getting professionals to meet with you. This approach has been tested with students for more than ten years and it helps you to be both persistent and respectful.

ACTION ITEMS

1. Begin contacting people in your warm network.

2. Begin the outreach process with five people from your list of twenty-five strategic contacts identified during step 2, and continue using the process until you either get a response or complete each action item in the ten-day outreach strategy. If you don't get a response, or if you get a hard no, *stop* contacting the professional.

Preparation—Strategies and Best Practices for Career Conversations

How would you prepare if you knew that tomorrow you would meet someone that would change your life?

—DAN CASETTA

Think about that quote. How would you prepare if you knew that tomorrow you would meet someone who would change your life? Career conversations sometimes become these life-changing meetings. This was Isaac's experience, and he was ready for his opportunity.

Isaac was a senior majoring in political science, Spanish, and ethnic studies, and he held a leadership position in a multicultural club at his school. Although he spent his time developing valuable leadership skills through the club, he didn't think much about his future career. He had worked hard to get a large scholarship as a first-generation student, but until he took my class, no one had talked to him about how to transition from college to a full-time job.

One of the professionals on Isaac's list of strategic contacts was a director of legal affairs for a state medical association. After two emails and a phone call, Isaac and the professional scheduled a career conversation via video chat.

In preparation for the meeting, Isaac resolved to learn as much as he could about this professional. Isaac looked him up on LinkedIn and learned that he was an attorney with experience in nonprofits and that he liked basketball. Isaac loved basketball himself, and he made a mental note to bring up the subject during their conversation. He kept his preparation focused by reminding himself of his goals: to build a relationship and to explore career options.

On Isaac's big day, he intentionally brought up basketball at the beginning of the conversation, and it ended up being a great conversation starter. During the conversation, Isaac learned that the professional's son played basketball, so he asked a few follow-up questions. He also talked about his favorite team, the Phoenix Suns.

The conversation lasted two hours. Isaac's genuine intention to learn about the director's career showed through, and the two chatted about a wide range of work- and non-work-related topics. As the conversation progressed, the man began asking Isaac about his passions and goals. The chat had turned into a quasi-interview on the spot.

STEP | 1 | 2 | 3 | 4 | **5** | 6 | 7 | 8 |

Isaac was prepared for this twist because he had already learned step 8 of the Career Launch Method, but he didn't think it would actually happen during the career conversation.

Then, at the end of the "interview," the man said, "You know, Isaac, I really like you. I'm going to make sure you have a job by the time you graduate in five months."

Isaac was beyond excited.

He and the director emailed back and forth several times over the next few weeks, with Isaac updating the director on his job search process and the director discussing new opportunities he found. About a month later, the director told Isaac that he could secure Isaac a formal job interview for a political consulting company. The man had given the company a strong recommendation of Isaac and told Isaac he would have a great shot at being hired.

Following an interview at the political consulting firm, one of the partners offered Isaac the job! Isaac resonated with the organization's mission to help represent communities like the one in which Isaac grew up. The job would be a great stepping-stone to a career in law, politics, or nonprofit work.

Within a few weeks, Isaac went from being unprepared for life after college to earning a job in the hidden job market—a job that aligned with his ikigai!

Isaac's preparation had played a key role in landing him an excellent job from a single career conversation. His attention to detail, effective use of small talk, authenticity, and humility had led him to gain not only a great job but also a new mentoring relationship.

Before you conduct a career conversation, you'll want to be prepared with questions and a strategy to make the most of the opportunity. Although over time you will become more confident having career conversations, your proficiency should never

 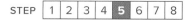

be an excuse to stop taking the time and effort to be prepared. Every career conversation is a chance to learn about an organization, a specific job role, and someone's distinct career path. But to maximize your learning during the conversation, you need to acquire as much relevant information as possible beforehand.

The obvious point of a career conversation is to learn about someone's career experiences, and this is important. However, the less obvious but equally important goal of your meeting is to *start a relationship with that individual that can develop over time.* This certainly won't happen with every career conversation, but you can take intentional steps during the initial conversation to build a more long-term relationship. Isaac's story is a great example of how an initial career conversation can lead to a valuable long-term connection.

While you are having your career conversation, look for signs that the other person is engaged. For example, your conversation might go so well that it goes longer than the scheduled time frame. Or you might find that you have commonalities with the other person. Either of these can be a signal that the person may be open to helping you more in the future. Keep in mind that a long-term relationship doesn't have to require a large time investment; it could be as simple as you asking for advice about an important career decision once or twice each year.

I'll cover tips on how to build long-lasting mentoring relationships through effective follow-up in step 7, but for now, just be aware that your goal isn't just to get information from someone; it's to build a more durable connection. In this section, we're focused on preparation—formulating specific questions and getting all the details right. Being prepared also means attending to your attire, body language, energy level, attitude, and timeliness. Mastering these details will enable you to make a good first impression and create an authentic connection.

We don't always rise to our highest expectations; most of the time we fall to our level of preparation.

—PARAPHRASE OF ARCHILOCHUS

KEY TAKEAWAY #1: ASK THE RIGHT QUESTIONS

Career conversations are quite different than a casual hangout with a friend. It's your responsibility to come prepared with a set of questions to guide the conversation and to demonstrate to the professional that you value their time. Career conversations provide a safe environment to learn about—and test any assumptions you have about—a company, role, and career path.

Some of your career conversations may take unexpected turns; for example, you may discover similar interests or share experiences with the other person. Your goal isn't to precisely plan the conversation ahead of time, but you should be prepared to lead and to ask questions that show you have done your homework in finding out what you can about the people with whom you are talking, their job function, and their organization. This starts with making small talk at the beginning of the conversation. Small talk is conversation about things unrelated to the key purpose of the meeting. You'll want to ask a strategic question or two to maximize the effectiveness of your small talk, as opposed to talking about the weather, for example.

You should spend at least one hour, usually more, preparing for each career conversation. Your career questions will be guided by your curiosity, your goals, and your research. If you are trying to learn more about a particular career path, you should ask about that. If you are interested in a certain organization, direct your questions toward the professional's experience working at that organization.

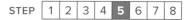

It's always a good idea to begin by finding out what you can about the person you will be meeting (such as what can you find on LinkedIn) and taking notes about their past experience. Some things you may want to put in your notes include:

- How long have they been in their position?

- Have they changed roles or even industries throughout their career?

- Where did they go to school and what did they study in college?

- What stage of their career are they in?

- What companies or people do they follow?

- Do they share anything about their interests or hobbies?

- How do they describe themselves?

- How did they get to where they are now?

This is not an exhaustive list, but questions like these will help you get a background on who they are and their career path.

Some employees will have biographies on their organization's website. Even if you can't find a specific employee's bio, you should always have a solid understanding of their organization before the conversation. For example:

- What industry is it in?

- How big is the organization?

- What products or services does it provide?

- Who are its customers, partners, and/or beneficiaries?

- What is the organization's mission?

- What words and terms are industry jargon?

You also can look for websites, blogs, or professional social media profiles of both the person and the organization. You often can learn what someone values based on their social media posts on sites like LinkedIn or Twitter.

Be prepared to spend the time necessary to find out as much information as you can in advance of the conversation. *If you put in this effort beforehand, you won't be wasting time asking about things that you should already know, and you will demonstrate your respect for the other person's time.* In addition, being armed with this background information will enable you to ask more meaningful questions during the conversation and be viewed as serious about your future career. Conversely, if you're unfocused and you haven't planned, you risk offending the professional and the potential to build an ongoing relationship.

Intentional Small Talk

Begin with questions that are not about career or jobs. Before jumping into your questions about someone's career path or organization, you should spend a few minutes on small talk or on asking simple, open-ended questions to establish a personal connection before jumping into your career-focused questions. Small talk ensures that your conversation feels like a genuine human connection, not just an exchange of information—or worse yet, an interrogation. Although small talk feels foreign or scary to many students, you can follow a simple method to start a conversation on a positive note. Making small talk is less about what you say than how you respond to the other person's statements and answers.

Start with "How's your day going?" This question is a standard way to begin a conversation. If the person gives a longer, thirty-second answer, feel free to give an answer that is about that length. The person might also give a short answer, like "Fine, thanks. How about you?" In this case, mirror the length of their answer by saying, "Fine, thanks."

Ask a question based on your research about them as a person (if applicable). Touching on a topic besides work allows you to build a more authentic connection. If you've taken note of a hobby or interest, you can ask about that. Note: Don't dig deep into someone's Facebook or non-professional profiles, because this could feel intrusive. However, anything mentioned on the person's employee biography, LinkedIn profile, or personal website is fair game.

For example, you might say, "I saw on your employee bio that you love to read biographies. Which book have you read most recently?"

Ask, "Do you have a time limit for this conversation?" I advise asking in your outreach email for only twenty minutes, but some people might block out half an hour or longer for the conversation. You can say, "I want to make sure I'm respectful of your time. I asked for twenty minutes. Do we have a hard stop in twenty minutes, or might we have a few additional minutes?" They may say yes or "I have thirty minutes blocked out" or simply "No, I have a hard stop." Knowing your time limit will help you prioritize asking your most important questions.

Provide one minute of background on yourself. Relationships are a two-way street, so while you should spend most of your time asking the professional questions, sharing a little bit of background information about yourself and what you're most interested in helps them get to know you and to be more helpful to you. The important thing is to keep your background information to about one minute.

Feel free to share any parts of your background or identity that you feel are important (you're a first-generation student, a student athlete, a transfer student, participate in student groups, or whatever seems appropriate). You also can briefly highlight one of your accomplishments or leadership experiences (such as "I'm really active in the environmental club at my college and I'm currently working on a weeklong event to spread awareness about climate change"). Make sure to touch on why you are excited to be speaking to the person and why you are interested in learning about their career path. Finish your background information by asking the other person a question, likely the career path question, which I will detail next.

If you know you only have twenty minutes, you might want to keep your small talk brief, but these types of questions can be key to developing ongoing relationships. Note: If the conversation goes well and you run out of time, you will likely have another opportunity to connect.

> *Telling creates resistance. Asking creates relationships.*
>
> —ANDREW SORBEL

Ask Smart, Meaningful Questions

The questions you ask say a lot about your levels of preparation and curiosity. You want to appear both knowledgeable and willing to learn. Here are examples of questions you might consider asking during your career conversations.

Career path question: "Can you walk me through some of your career path, starting with your experiences in college at [name their college], including any work or internships you had?"

This question lets the other person share the relevant details of their career path and how they ended up in their current job. It also shows that you did some research about their background and education. After someone answers this question, ask

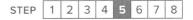

a follow-up question about a part of their answer that you found interesting or even confusing.

Job questions:

- What does your typical day/week look like?

- What do you like most about your work? What are you excited about right now?

- What is challenging about your work? Which aspects don't you enjoy?

- What skills are most important for a job like yours?

- What questions or problem are you trying to solve?

Organization questions:

- How would you describe the culture at [Company/Organization Name]? How is the culture (values and norms) different from others in your industry or from your previous employers?

- What does your organization do to provide resources and opportunities to employees from diverse backgrounds?

- What kinds of professional development and/or mentorship does [Company/Organization Name] provide?

Industry questions:

- What advice would you give your younger self starting out in the industry?

- What do you think is the best way to find an internship (or job) in this field or industry?

■ What didn't you know before you got into this industry, that you wish someone had told you?

Closing questions. In step 6, I'll discuss the questions you should ask at the end of your career conversation based on your desired outcome.

> *When people talk, listen completely. . . . Most people never listen.*
>
> —ERNEST HEMINGWAY

Active Listening and Authentic Connections

Though I've spoken about the importance of being prepared, you should always prioritize being natural and authentic over sticking to your list of questions. Asking questions based on what the person is saying shows that you are actively listening and engaged in the conversation. You don't need to have a rigid order to your questions. Be willing to switch the order based on the direction of the conversation and what you want to learn.

For example, perhaps you want to ask a question about the culture of the organization, and this is the fourth question on your list. If they begin talking about their experience at the organization while answering your first question, you can ask your question about culture next. You should start by rephrasing a key takeaway from the person's answer to show that you understood them. For example, "Thanks for sharing that. It sounds like relationships with your colleagues were really meaningful during that project, and this seems reflective of your organization's culture. How would you describe the culture in your workplace?" Active listening is crucial to building an authentic connection that has the potential to continue long after your initial conversation.

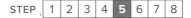

If a question doesn't feel right, don't ask it. If the conversation goes off topic and you don't get to ask all your questions, that's okay. Again, if you end up having a great discussion and run out of time without asking some of your main questions, the person likely will be open to a follow-up conversation. Remember, your goal is to build a relationship, not to squeeze eight questions into twenty minutes. Most of the time, the conversation ends with the professional welcoming you to keep in touch, so you likely will have more chances to ask questions.

> *There's no magic in magic; it's all in the details.*
>
> —WALT DISNEY

KEY TAKEAWAY #2: UNDERSTAND PROPER ETIQUETTE

Etiquette is a collection of small behaviors that allow you to make a strong first impression. Taken together, the habits that I describe here will result in other people seeing you as the kind of person they would like to support—and as a person they would recommend to others, or even consider hiring, if the opportunity presented itself. After all, what employer isn't looking for people who present themselves as competent, prepared, engaged, proactive, and thoughtful?

These tips apply to in-person meetings, video chats, and phone calls, though I've added some details specific to video chats and phone calls near the end.

What to Wear

For most industries, wear professional or business casual attire (no t-shirts, sweatshirts, sweatpants, or hats). This holds true for in-person meetings, video calls, and even phone calls (it puts

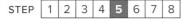

you in the right mindset). Ideally, have a general idea about the level of professionalism for the organization or industry where you are interviewing. For example, a nonprofit may have an informal workplace, whereas a bank might be more formal and a hospital has employees wearing uniforms. If you're unsure about anything, it's always better to err on the side of being more professionally dressed than less. You can also contact a career counselor or professor for advice.

What to Bring

For an in-person meeting, it's a good idea to bring a laptop or tablet, just in case it might come in handy. Perhaps there will be something you could show about your work or experience, if appropriate. Also, bring some sort of professional looking folder that includes a pad to take notes and space where you can store a few copies of your résumé, ideally printed on thick card stock paper. The professional may ask you for a copy, so you should be prepared if they do.

For a video meeting, you can take notes on a pad of paper. Taking a few notes is a good idea, whether in person or not, because it sends a signal to the other person both that you are listening and that they are saying something that you find important enough to jot down. But don't take notes the whole time; you should avoid looking down for extended periods. It's important to maintain good eye contact, even on a video chat. Typing notes can be viewed as distracting and is not ideal in some situations.

When to Arrive

If you are driving to an in-person meeting at an office, I suggest arriving at the parking lot twenty to thirty minutes early. If you are taking public transportation or using a rideshare service, make sure to anticipate possible delays and give yourself an extra cushion of at least twenty minutes. You should enter the office lobby about ten minutes early, because you often will have to speak to a receptionist and go through some check-in procedure before going past the lobby.

For a video call, I suggest logging on two to five minutes early. Just don't be late! Your timeliness shows that you respect the other person's schedule and helps you create a positive impression. For a phone call, make the call at the exact time you agreed on.

Nonverbal Communication

Nonverbal communication describes the behaviors and body language that form a major part of communications. Sometimes what is said matters less than how it is said. First, make sure to smile, even for phone calls. Occasionally smiling shows that you are engaged and interested and creates warmth. Maintain good posture, sitting up straight with your shoulders back. Make good eye contact with the other person.

Your speaking tone is also essential. You might want to ask family or friends for feedback about how you come across in conversations. If you are normally energetic and engaged, this might be easy. However, if you are naturally more shy or subdued, you should consider making additional effort to show your energy, enthusiasm, and interest during career conversations.

Finish Strong

At the end of the conversation, regardless of how well you feel it went, you should express your gratitude. Always thank the person for their time and for sharing their experiences and insights.

In the next section, I'll cover the strategic questions to ask at the end of your conversation, and some follow-up steps, but as a baseline, you should always be saying thank you and telling the person that the conversation has been meaningful to you. Mentioning *why* it has been meaningful would be even better!

Video Chats

Due to the Covid-19 pandemic, video chats have become common in a wide variety of industries. Although our research has demonstrated that they still aren't quite as good as in-person meetings, they are much better than phone calls for building long-term relationships.

During video calls, you should be aware of what can be seen in your background. Don't be too close or too far away from the camera. Make sure your room is well lit and that your face can be seen clearly. Look directly into the camera when you're speaking, as this provides the best sense of eye contact with the other person. Make sure that your location is quiet and free of any distracting sounds or background noises.

Phone Calls

Some professionals will want to talk with you on the phone, perhaps while they are commuting, or for any number of other reasons. Although this is not ideal, you can make the most of a phone conversation. First, understand that without body language or facial expressions, the tone of your voice and your enthusiasm are essential for phone calls. Speak clearly and vary the ups and downs of your sentences to convey enthusiasm. Talk at a steady pace—not too fast or too slow.

I suggest standing up and even walking around a room if it helps you stay engaged. Alternatively, phone calls make it easier to take notes, especially if you use headphones or earbuds, which is recommended. Make sure that your location is quiet and free of any distracting sounds or background noises.

REVIEW AND REFLECT

- Every career conversation requires preparation. You should perform background research and identify the main questions you want to ask for every career conversation.

- Your goal in a career conversation is to develop a longer-term relationship. Making a good first impression, asking a few small talk questions, and practicing active listening can help you build an authentic connection.

- Visualize being asked to talk about yourself at the beginning of a career conversation. Practice giving a short answer and finishing with a question about the professional.

- Attend to the small details that can make a difference. For example, be on time, take a few notes, smile, and express gratitude.

- Think about these questions as part of your preparation: What do you hope to get out of career conversations? What aspects of career conversations are you most confident about? Most nervous about?

- Reflect on the etiquette tips. What aspects do you need to be mindful of?

ACTION ITEMS

Before every career conversation, you should do the following:

1. Conduct research and learn about the professional's career, where they have worked, their hobbies, interests, and so on. Put your findings in your notes.

2. Write down or type out a list of questions you want to prioritize for each conversation.

Advanced Preparation— Turning Career Conversations into Interviews, Recommendations, and Referrals

Luck is what happens when preparation meets opportunity.

—SENECA

One month before the start of her senior year, Sonya had to make a decision. The accounting company where she had recently interned had offered her a full-time position after graduation. However, ever since she was a sophomore, her heart had been set on working for Cornerstone Research. Unfortunately, Cornerstone Research chose not to display its entry-level jobs on her school's online job posting platform, nor did Cornerstone attend her school's career fairs or host information sessions, because her school was not one of the company's "target schools." Now Sonya had less than four weeks before she needed to accept or decline her accounting offer.

As a sophomore, Sonya had felt confident in choosing finance as a major, but she wasn't sure what career her interests would lead to. She figured she would explore career options online and ask professionals about their experiences. She attended conferences and information sessions hosted by larger accounting firms. She conducted career conversations with professionals from a variety of industries, asking to learn more about their career paths.

Now, as a senior applying to Cornerstone, she sent initial emails to current and former professionals at the organization, but no one responded. Next, Sonya sent the "Day 3" follow-up emails. This time she got a response from someone who turned out to be a hiring manager, and she scheduled a career conversation for the following week. By asking the right questions during her conversation, Sonya was able to turn this new relationship into a formal interview.

Was Sonya surprised? No, she was shocked! She hadn't expected her plan to work out. The interview process went well, and Sonya received a full-time offer from her dream company before the decision deadline for her other offer!

Sonya told me that the key breakthrough was her decision to put her full effort into creating relationships with employees at her desired organization. Although she knew the odds weren't in her favor with such a short timeline and not being from a target school, her proactive approach paid off.

STEP | 1 | 2 | 3 | 4 | 5 | **6** | 7 | 8 |

"You've got to step out of your comfort zone and be proactive, even if you think it won't succeed," she said. "The common route won't work for most people. The odds are stacked against most students. If I hadn't learned the Career Launch Method, I wouldn't have pursued Cornerstone or gotten the interview, let alone land the job."

One reason for Sonya's success is that she engaged in career education and exploration throughout her time in college. Early on, her goal was simply to learn about job types and industries to help with discernment. As a sophomore and junior, her goal was to land internships. As a senior, her goal was to get a job she really wanted. Importantly, Sonya understood how to effectively structure the endings of career conversations based on her desired outcome for each conversation.

> *If you don't know where you are going, you will probably end up somewhere else.*
>
> —LAWRENCE J. PETER

KEY TAKEAWAY #1: KNOW YOUR DESIRED RESULT FOR EACH CONVERSATION

Before conducting a career conversation, consider what you hope to get out of the conversation. For example, you may simply want to learn more about an industry, an organization, or a job function. You may want to learn about someone's career path to help with your exploration and discernment process. You may be looking to develop a mentor/mentee relationship. Perhaps you want an internal recommendation for a posting you saw online, or a referral to someone else in the organization. Or you might be looking to be invited to a formal interview for a job or internship.

Career conversations are effective for all these goals. However, you need to know your goal before conducting the conversation, because it will influence the questions you ask near the end and it will determine your follow-up strategy.

Note: For all career conversations it is a best practice to offer to be a resource to the professional. This gesture expresses your gratitude for their time and says you are willing to help out as a thank you for the conversation. You can simply say, "If there is a way I can be of help to you or the organization, please keep me in mind." Most of the time there will not be any follow-through, but I have had students participate in surveys and focus groups as a result of making the offer. Either way, your offer will reflect positively on your personal brand.

If your goal is to get a formal job interview, use this proven four-question sequence. Many professionals expect that you want a job or internship simply because you have set up the career conversation, so it's not a huge leap to ask about future job opportunities. But you want to adhere to some norms. It's like bringing dessert to a dinner party at someone's home. The guest brings dessert because the host is providing dinner, but it would be awkward for the guest to explicitly say, "I bought you this dessert because you paid for the groceries and made the dinner."

Similarly, professionals will expect that you asked for a conversation because you are interested in an internship or job, but you shouldn't explicitly talk about wanting the job at the beginning of the conversation. After all, you set up the meeting by asking to learn about their career path. However, it is totally acceptable to inquire toward the end. In fact, most professionals expect it. It's a social norm, like bringing dessert to a dinner party.

It is very important, then, to be strategic with your timing and transition into asking questions about internship or job opportunities. If you ask about a job at the beginning of the conversation, you look insincere and selfish. But the right questions near the end of the conversation can lead the professional to invite you to a formal interview or to refer you to the appropriate person.

In some cases, people will bring up job opportunities even if you don't ask. But don't count on it. Ask these four questions when you are ready to transition from the questions on your list to asking about a formal internship or job opportunity.

1. What qualities or characteristics do you and the organization look for in an ideal internship applicant (or entry-level employee, etc.)?

2. Can I take a minute to tell you a little more about myself? (Keep your answer to two minutes or less so the other person stays engaged. Try to use what they just said about ideal candidates in your description about yourself. If you have already spent a good amount of time talking about yourself because the professional asked you several questions, you can skip ahead to question 3.)

3. Based on what I've shared, do you think I'm someone who would be a good fit at this company/organization?

4. Who do you recommend I speak with about internship (or job) opportunities? What do you suggest would be my next steps?

If you don't get the opportunity to ask these questions during the career conversation, you can ask about job opportunities or connections to hiring managers in your follow-up emails. But your success rate is maximized if you do it in the concluding moments of your live conversation.

If your goal is to develop a mentor/mentee relationship . . .
career conversations are great ways to develop relationships with

 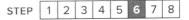

professionals who can be advisers and help you make important career decisions. Many students believe that to qualify as a mentor, someone has to be meeting with you frequently (like once a month) and discussing a whole range of life issues. This isn't true. You can have a variety of mentors with whom you speak only when you have an important decision, opportunity, question, or transition. And ironically, one of the best ways to build relationships with mentors is to *avoid* explicitly asking them to be your mentor.

If someone is a busy professional and you ask them "Will you be my mentor?," they might be hesitant because they believe it will require a large time investment on their part. But if you ask them about a specific and relevant topic (for instance, "I am pursuing internships in two different industries. Could I ask you a few questions for some advice?"), they are more likely to want to help you. By following up periodically over time, you can build trust and develop a mentoring relationship.

If your goal is to get a referral . . . almost all organizations have some method for employee referrals. Large companies often have online systems where employees can easily refer a candidate who has applied through their internal job portal. Most small and medium-size organizations operate without such formal structures, but they still encourage employees to make referrals to hiring managers or human resources.

Unless you feel like the professional you're meeting with is disinterested or the conversation is not going well, you should consider asking some or all of the following questions at the end of the conversation:

- I know we just met, but based on the little bit you know about me, would you be willing to recommend me as a candidate for an internship (or job)?

- Who do you know that would be helpful for me to connect with?

- If I receive a formal interview, would you be willing to put in a good word for me?

A study of more than two thousand employees indicated that, once interviewed, the chances of getting hired are *twelve times higher* for a candidate with a referral than for someone who only completed an online application.[1] This is why asking the question *Would you be willing to recommend me as a candidate for an internship (or job)?* can make such a major impact.

If your goal is simply to explore and learn about new career options . . . such as to learn about a particular career path, industry, company, or organization, there is little downside (and nearly unlimited upside) to asking for connections to other people. Try to be specific in your request. For example, perhaps you have a conversation with a teacher and you're also interested in becoming a principal down the road. Rather than asking whether the person knows anyone who could help you, you might ask if they would be willing to introduce you to the principal at their school for a conversation. Also, you can say, "Would you mind if I stay in touch periodically?" You will likely receive an affirmation and will open the door for future communication.

You have to be explicit and clear in asking for what you want. During career conversations, some professionals may proactively offer to refer you to colleagues for further conversations, or even ask you to apply for an internship or job. But these cases are more the exception than the norm. Most of the time, you will need to ask for what you want. Many professionals will only help you if you explicitly ask, not because they are testing you or withholding anything but just because they aren't sure what you want.

If you use the recommended outreach templates given in step 4, you will be saying that you have an assignment to conduct a career conversation. Although this improves your odds of getting a response, the person you speak with may think that you are just trying to complete your assignment. They may not realize you have a great interest in securing an internship or job, an ongoing relationship, or a referral. Again, therefore, you must explicitly ask for what you want.

I've had many students over the years follow 90% of the Career Launch Method and then fail to ask for a connection or to inquire about internship or job opportunities before ending the interaction. You don't want to be part of this group, because that means you are not maximizing your chances for success. It's your responsibility to ask about next steps and who else would be good for you to speak with. The questions presented here will put you in the best possible position to turn a career conversation into something more.

> *To expect the unexpected shows a thoroughly modern intellect.*
>
> —OSCAR WILDE

KEY TAKEAWAY #2: EXPECT THE UNEXPECTED

You should be prepared for a wide variety of outcomes during your career conversation. Although some of these scenarios are rare, it's always best to be prepared. My first tip is to visualize the conversation the night before. Start by thinking about how you want the professional to feel about you when conversation is over. How will they perceive you? Consider what kind of energy, emotion, and state of being you'll embody during the chat. What can you do, verbally and nonverbally, to give yourself the best chance for the conversation to turn into something

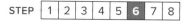

more? Taking just a few minutes to close your eyes and visualize your intended outcome can work wonders to make you more focused and effective.

Now, certainly, not all career conversations will be life changing. But as you can see from the student stories in this book, it happens more often than you might imagine. It's part of the reason why 80% of jobs are never advertised. In general, professionals like to help students who reach out, so they likely already have a positive impression of you before your meeting. Then, when you create an authentic connection, you cultivate job search gravity, making positive outcomes more likely.

Here are some scenarios for which you should prepare.

- **Length of conversation.** Some people will have a hard stop at the twenty minutes you asked for, and others won't. Some people will block off thirty or even sixty minutes. This is why I advocate asking whether the person has a time limit at the beginning of the conversation. Often, if the person has time and the conversation is going well, it can go longer than your allotted time, which is terrific. Be grateful and respectful of the person's time, regardless of length.

- **Your professional shows up late, fails to show, or reschedules.** Do not let this affect your attitude or disposition. Try not to act disappointed, frustrated, or even angry, and maintain your enthusiasm and respect. You never know what someone else is working on, and you should be grateful that they are taking the time to meet with you. If you are holding a video or phone call and five minutes pass without your hearing anything, you can assume that something came up for the other person, and you should politely make the effort to reschedule the conversation. The good news is that if this happens, the person will likely be even more responsive and will appreciate your graciousness. Send an email similar to the following template.

Subject line: Need to reschedule?

Hi, [Name],

Do you need a few more minutes to jump on our call, or would you prefer to reschedule for another day?

Thanks,
[Your Name]

- **Other people unexpectedly join the conversation.** If you are having an in-person meeting, it's possible that other people could join your conversation or that you could meet new people while walking around the office. One of my former students, Marcus, had a career conversation with the former chief financial officer of Netflix. At the end of the discussion, the CFO said, "Aren't you going to ask me for a tour?" If you are meeting in person, always ask for a tour. You'll get a better feel for the organization's culture and you are likely to be introduced to other professionals along the way, with whom you may be able to schedule a subsequent conversation. For instance, I had a student, Lisa, who had a career conversation at Yelp, and during her office tour she met a Yelp manager in the elevator who gave her his business card. She followed up with him, got a formal interview, and landed a summer internship!

- **On-the-spot interview.** During some career conversations, professionals might ask you questions about your interests or experiences. You should always be ready to answer these interview-style questions. I'll share some best practices on how to prepare for interviews in step 8.

- **Asked for a copy of your résumé.** If you are meeting in person, you should bring three or four copies of your résumé

to distribute in the event that you are asked. If you are meeting via video chat, your résumé should be updated so that it can be emailed.

The bottom line from all these scenarios is that you should go with the flow and be flexible. Most times, these unexpected circumstances will benefit you if you are prepared and adaptable. All these scenarios can serve as a bridge between a career conversation and a formal interview, if that is your desired outcome. Regardless of your goal, though, mental preparation can give you a greater shot at success.

REVIEW AND REFLECT

- Know your desired result for your career conversation, which might be to land an internship or job, create a mentoring relationship, get a referral or recommendation, or explore new career options. Based on your goal, be prepared to ask the right questions *at the end* of the conversation. Be clear about asking for what you want.

- Consider the activities and conversations you have scheduled for tomorrow and the near future. Then think about the people involved and how you want those people to feel after you interact with them. Finally, think about what kind of energy, emotion, and state of being you'll need to embody to create your intended outcome.

- "Expect the unexpected" by mentally preparing for a wide variety of outcomes for your career conversation and being ready to adapt accordingly.

ACTION ITEMS

1. Write down your goal(s) for each career conversation before the meeting.

2. If you want to inquire about an internship or job, practice the four-question sequence out loud.

3. If you want a recommendation and/or to be referred to someone else, practice the questions from that section out loud.

Effective Follow-Up— Differentiate Yourself and Build Long-Term Relationships

People will forget what you said. People will forget what you did. But people will never forget how you made them feel.

—MAYA ANGELOU

Andrew played basketball in college, which meant that he didn't have time during summers for internships. As a result, he didn't have a clear idea of what he wanted to do as a career. During his senior year, in 2015, Andrew applied online to a wide variety of jobs but found it challenging to get interviews.

Of the few interviews he did receive, none resulted in a job offer. Companies would typically tell him, "Thanks for your interest, but we went with someone who had more experience."

Andrew needed a job after graduation, so he persevered and made it to the final round of interviews for a sales position, meeting with a manager named Maria. Although Andrew felt good about how the interview went, he received an email several days later from the company's recruiter informing him that they would not be making him a job offer. Andrew was dismayed, but he reached out to the recruiter and asked for the hiring manager's email so that he could thank her for the consideration. In his email, Andrew thanked Maria for her time and asked if she could provide any feedback on how to improve.

Andrew received a long message from Maria with detailed feedback about his interview. She explained that Andrew had performed well and was a strong candidate for the position but that there were several areas for improvement. For example, she suggested that Andrew could have asked questions about the company and team at the end of the interview. In addition, since Andrew was applying for a sales position, Maria was looking for him to be more relaxed and confident during the interview. She also indicated that Andrew could have been more forthcoming in asking about next steps during the interview.

However, crucially for Andrew, Maria concluded with this line, "I do have other sales manager colleagues that may/may not have openings, so let me know if you would like an introduction to them for a conversation." Andrew promptly responded with gratitude for the feedback and said that he would love an introduction. He didn't hear from Maria for about a week, so Andrew sent her a follow-up email mentioning that he had seen an open position at the company on an online job board. This time, Maria responded, said that she appreciated Andrew's persistence, and connected him to another hiring manager, Scott. Andrew had a phone call with Scott and then received an in-person interview the following week. At the end of this interview, Scott offered him a job, and Andrew joined the organization shortly afterward. Andrew's effective follow-up transformed a rejection into a job!

Andrew and I spoke while I was writing this book, and he shared how effective follow-up had landed him another job in 2020. After several years in sales positions, Andrew had become a successful account executive at a large company, but he wanted to try his hand at a smaller, early-stage company. The timing of this change could not have been worse. The organization had to make some dramatic shifts in response to the COVID-19 pandemic, and after only a few months on the job, Andrew's position was eliminated.

> *Success is stumbling from failure to failure with no loss of enthusiasm.*
>
> —WINSTON CHURCHILL

Andrew told me that he once again used the Career Launch Method, making a top ten list and doing outreach. He sent an email to an alumnus who was the senior vice president at a company he thought would be a good match. After their career conversation, Andrew followed up and asked if the VP could put him in touch with a hiring manager. Over email, the VP asked for his résumé and made a referral for Andrew. After several interviews, Andrew was hired.

Andrew's story shows that effective follow-up can be even more critical than a career conversation or formal interview. I find that students too often fail to realize the power of following up. There is almost always a polite way to continue the relationship.

Note: as someone with many years of hiring experience, I can add that effective follow-up sometimes is the difference maker when choosing between two equally qualified candidates.

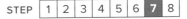

As a senior, Andrew had been applying through online job portals for months, but he wasn't able to land a job until he embraced a holistic job search that included a focus on career conversations. His efforts created a relationship that, despite rejection, eventually led to a job offer.

In steps 4–6, we, we discussed that the goal of your career conversations is not just to learn but also to build a relationship. When it comes to building relationships, follow-up is essential.

Think about the difference between the experiences of two students looking for jobs around the time of their graduation. The first student never had a career conversation or gave much thought to what she wanted to do with her life, and so she was primarily applying to jobs online and trying to catch up by networking as much as possible. Her counterpart started doing career conversations during her sophomore year and followed up with these professionals occasionally throughout college. After doing an average of ten career conversations per year for three years, she had amassed a network of thirty professionals in her fields of interest to whom she could reach out about positions. If this student was interested in one of the companies where she had already started a relationship with an employee, she would be in a great position to reach out to those people and ask them for a referral or connection to a hiring manager. She would not have to spend as much time applying to jobs online because she built her network before she needed it and then used follow-up requests to conduct her job search.

If you are a senior or have recently completed your degree or certificate and have not yet done any career conversations, it is not too late to start. Just look to Isaac's and Andrew's stories, and Ivanna's story in step 8. Obviously, however, starting early and occasionally following up with these professionals puts you in a more advantageous position to land a job you want upon completion of your schooling.

STEP 1 | 2 | 3 | 4 | 5 | 6 | **7** | 8

> *Two roads diverged in a wood, and I—*
> *I took the one less traveled by,*
> *And that has made all the difference.*
>
> —ROBERT FROST

KEY TAKEAWAY #1: SEPARATE YOURSELF FROM THE COMPETITION

When she responded to Andrew's request for interview feedback, Maria told him that he was one of only a handful of candidates in her eighteen-year career who had asked for feedback. With his thank-you email and simple request, Andrew had separated himself from the competition and showed that he was the sort of person (employee) who was dedicated to self-improvement. Note that it is not best practice to ask for feedback *during* an interview, because some employers view it as a lack of confidence, but it can be effective after you've been told you didn't get the job. When searching for jobs, you should always be on the lookout for ways to differentiate yourself.

The first step in being able to effectively follow up is to take notes. You should be taking some notes during the conversation, and as soon as the conversation or interview ends, you should write down all of your key takeaways. Psychologists have found that most people forget about 40% of what they have heard just twenty minutes after a conversation.[1] That number increases to forgetting 70% one day later. To counteract this human process, you should take notes, which will be helpful in constructing your follow-up messages and building relationships.

There are three main considerations when taking notes.

1. Write down specific details associated with organization names, important people, or key events from the stories you hear. These details often come in handy later.

2. Write down any informal, non-work-related topics that were discussed, such as hobbies, interests, books, sports teams, or shared experiences. I find that many students neglect to write down these topics because they do not seem critical to learning about careers, but you'll see that they will come in handy for the messages in the "Keeping Relationships Alive" section.

3. Finally, you should jot down the key takeaways and lessons learned (those which are most helpful or inspiring) from the conversation. These will come in handy, especially when you prepare your thank-you messages.

Your next step is to send an email to the individual with whom you had a career conversation, first thing the next morning (preferably between 6:00 and 7:00 a.m.).

I know that there are ways to schedule your email, but there are two reasons why you should send it manually. First, I've had multiple students tell me they used the scheduling feature and accidentally sent their follow-up emails a week later instead of the next morning. Second, some companies have software that will flag emails that are sent using a scheduling feature, which defeats part of the purpose.

I advocate sending the email early in the morning to show that you are an early riser who is reflective. Professionals notice the time stamp on incoming emails, and this will positively impact your personal brand. It also is best practice, when you have an important but not urgent email to write, to "sleep on it." If your natural tendency is to fire off a thank-you email hours after a meeting, or a few days later, I encourage you to consider this "next morning" timeline.

Hanna, a former student studying physical therapy in Pennsylvania, sent her thank-you email at 6:45 a.m., received a

9:00 a.m. phone call from an impressed hiring manager acknowledging her early morning email, and then got another phone call that day at 4:00 p.m. with a job offer.

In your thank-you email, you should express gratitude for the professional's time and include one of the key takeaways from your notes. Rather than being generic ("Thank you for helping me"), be specific ("Your insights on the difference between account manager and account executive roles will be really helpful in my job search process"). The template below can help you shape your thank-you email.

> Subject line: Thank you from [Your Name]
>
> Dear [Name],
>
> It was great to talk with you yesterday. I really appreciate your making time for me, and I appreciated learning about your experiences. In particular, I enjoyed what you said about _____. I need to give that more thought as I transition from college into a career.
>
> It was also great to learn about _____. I appreciate your advice. I'll certainly be mindful of that going forward. [Or "I'll start working on that right away."]
>
> Thank you for encouraging me to stay in touch [and offering to introduce me to _____].
>
> I have attached my résumé to this email. I would appreciate your keeping me in mind for any positions that would be a good fit.
>
> Again, many thanks.
> [Your Name]

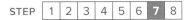

Sending a thank-you email is an important step, but I also highly recommend sending a handwritten thank-you note if you know the address where the person works. If you know that the person you spoke with is working from home and you don't know their address, you can skip this step, but handwritten notes are one of the best ways to differentiate yourself from the mass of applicants. Countless former students have told me their handwritten thank-you note was a difference-maker. Yuho, was one of two thousand applicants for two available positions with Adidas in Japan in early 2021, was explicity told that her handwritten thank-you note was one of the reasons she got her full-time job.

Below is a template for your handwritten thank-you notes.

Dear [Name],

Thanks again for your time [*earlier this week/last week*]. I've already [*started thinking about* _____, *or started doing* _____] and I'm excited about _____.

Learning about [*be specific, not general, about one of the main things you learned*] was really valuable. I'll certainly keep that in mind as I prepare to launch my career.

With much appreciation,
[Your Name]

Below is a template for how to address a letter to a company or organization.

[Organization Name]
Attn: [Recipient Name]
[Recipient Job Title]
500 Main St.
City, State [and] Zip Code

> *A mentor is someone who allows you see the hope*
> *inside yourself.*
>
> —OPRAH WINFREY

KEY TAKEAWAY #2: KEEP THE RELATIONSHIP ALIVE

You don't want to reach out to someone only when you need them—you want to build an enduring relationship. Think about your friendships: if someone always asked for your help but never gave anything back to you in return, your friendship would neither be strong nor survive for very long. Networking with professionals is obviously different, because you are speaking with people who have more experience than you do. However, if you have maintained a casual relationship over time, you're more likely to receive a prompt and thorough response from the person when you get back in touch with a specific question or request.

Many students mistakenly think that keeping a relationship alive requires an enormous investment of time and energy. On the contrary, your follow-up messages not only *can* be short and simple but also *should* be short and simple. Keeping in touch just a few times over the year is generally enough to keep the relationship alive. It is not best practice to reach out more than once every few months *unless* you get the sense that the person is excited to engage with you because of some mutual interests and/or common concerns.

Unlike your career conversation requests, these follow-up messages should not end with a question, unless you have established a strong interpersonal relationship. This might sound counterintuitive, but let me explain. If you ask someone in your message "How are you doing?," they may avoid responding because it would require time to prepare a thoughtful answer. When you send a note that doesn't include a question, it simply reminds them of your conversation and what you've been doing since or thinking about. You don't burden them with the necessity of taking much time to acknowledge and/or respond to your note. Yet your goal is accomplished: you've stayed in touch, they think positively of you, and they'll be more inclined to help you in the future when you have a request.

Another common objection that I hear from students is that they don't know what to say in a follow-up message. To make this action as easy as possible, here are three frameworks for sending messages in an effort to build long-term relationships.

1. The "Thought of You" Method

As the name suggests, this type of message is sent to tell someone that you were reminded of them based on something from your conversation. For example, maybe you have a professor who speaks about the professional's industry or job function during class. Or maybe you discussed a common love of science fiction books during your career conversation. After class, or the next time you finish a science fiction book, you can send them a short message saying that it made you think of them.

This also works well with online articles. Perhaps you saw an article celebrating an achievement of the person's company or an article about a topic from your conversation, either related or unrelated to career. You can email them the article and say that it reminded you of something that the two of you had discussed.

Remember, most of the time it is better to end these messages by writing something like "Hope you're doing well" than with a question. You'll be more likely to get a response, and it's better for your personal brand.

2. The Reflection and Gratitude Method

Another easy way to keep in touch with professionals is by sending messages around key milestones in the calendar, such as the end of the quarter/semester or academic year or holidays such as Thanksgiving and New Year's. In these messages, you can say that you have been reflecting on your conversation and continue to be grateful that they made themselves available to talk with you. Your message could be something like, "As I finish my junior year, I was reflecting on what I learned from our conversation and wanted to thank you again for taking the time to give me advice on my career [*or job search or the like*]. I hope you are doing well." Or, "During this time of Thanksgiving, I've thought about how grateful I am for you taking the time to meet with me earlier this year and providing me with your perspective and guidance. Happy holidays."

If there are more than a handful of people with whom you want to build longer-term relationships, it can be difficult to keep track of when you have reached out to people. The great thing about this method is that you can keep a list of everyone you want to follow up with and send all these messages around your chosen timelines.

3. The Social Media Method

This method relies on social media to form brief connections that keep you at the top of their minds. I'll refer to LinkedIn here, but other social media networks, like Twitter or Instagram, also may work, depending on the person, their industry, and what is most appropriate. If the professional posts on LinkedIn, you can comment on their post. If they have commented on someone else's post, you can reply to their comments. Most people don't look at everyone who has simply liked a post, but commenting, often quite briefly, does often get noticed and shows that you are engaged. It will help you keep the relationship alive.

Many professionals maintain an active presence on LinkedIn even if they don't regularly post or comment. In this case, you can share a relevant post or article with them through a private message. Share the link and a few sentences about why you thought the post or article would be of interest to them, again linking back to your overlapping interests. And again, do not end with a question.

If you use these methods you will develop future allies, supporters, and champions. You don't want to think of career conversations as one-off meetings. Take the long view and build a relationship over time. If you are part of a student group or club, perhaps you can extend invitations to be a guest speaker or to a networking event. Building relationships can be tough when there is a wide age or professional gap, but if you focus on keeping the person apprised of your progress and you are seen as grateful, not constantly taking, it shows you listened and their advice mattered.

In preparation for this book, I conducted qualitative interviews with professionals whom my students had met with for career conversations. Consistently, the professionals told me they really enjoy hearing from students months and years after the initial career converation. Though, one woman shared with me that she never heard from my student after the thank-you email and handwritten thank-you note, which she said was a bummer because she would have offered the student an internship. She didn't feel it was her responsiblity to reach out to the student so she chose someone else. So, be sure to make time to keep your relationships alive.

REVIEW AND REFLECT

- Get into the habit of taking notes immediately after career conversations, interviews, and important meetings.

- You should always err on the side of being too appreciative. Send a thank-you email the first thing in the morning after any career conversations or interviews and mail a handwritten thank-you card.

- Keep your network alive by keeping in touch with the professionals you meet, so that you can build a relationship, and, when necessary, ask for advice and counsel. Use the Thought of You method, the Reflection and Gratitude method, and the Social Media method.

ACTION ITEMS

1. When you schedule a career conversation in your calendar, also make a note to send a thank-you email the following day, between 6:00 and 7:00 a.m.

2. Purchase a box of thank-you cards. Have them on hand and use them often.

3. Make a reoccurring quarterly/semiannual note in your calendar to reconnect with professionals and people in your network.

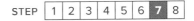

Ace the Job Interview— Convey Your Value and Land the Position

On the day of victory, no pain is felt.

—VINCE LOMBARDI

On her graduation day, Ivanna felt a mix of pride and apprehension. She had successfully earned a bachelor's degree in information technology and management from an excellent public university. However, she didn't have any internship experience and worried that she would struggle to find a full-time role. She actually had begun to look for employment toward the end of her senior year but didn't have any success.

Through a scholarship program with the Hispanic Foundation of Silicon Valley during the summer after graduation, Ivanna participated in a Career Launch program. During which, she reached out and scheduled a meeting with a senior product manager from Palo Alto Networks, the number one organization on her top ten list. She had already applied to a job posting online, so toward the end of the career conversation, Ivanna used the four-question sequence taught in step 6 to inquire about a formal interview. It worked, and the product manager recommended her for an interview.

Ivanna proceeded to go through eight interviews. There were behavioral interviews, group interviews, technical interviews, and a final-round interview where she had to deliver a presentation. Each of these steps was unfamiliar to Ivanna, but she took the initiative to reach out for help from mentors, including that senior product manager. Learning about the Career Launch Method empowered Ivanna to be more confident during the entire interview process and better prepared for each type of interview. Without any internship or work experience, she relied more heavily on classes and group projects to form her stories.

The weekend after her final-round presentation, Ivanna received an email from the recruiter: she would not be hired for the position. As you would expect, she was devastated, particularly after going through such a long process. However, Ivanna was determined to keep her head up and to persevere through this challenge. She reached out again to the senior product manager and learned that the company was hiring for a similar position in Texas, though this had not been formally advertised. Ivanna's networking had given her a second chance and a new opportunity in the hidden job market.

As Ivanna progressed through this second batch of interviews, she learned the importance of practicing the stories she wanted to tell when answering behavioral questions. She also learned about being honest when there was something she did not know in a technical interview. She asked smart questions and acted with professionalism throughout the process.

This time around, Ivanna landed the job as a systems engineer! Her diligence and hard work paid off. Through all of her interviews, Ivanna learned how to maintain emotional resilience in the face of failure, how to advocate for herself, and how to navigate the lengthy job interview process.

Ivanna's story demonstrates that career conversations are often complementary to traditional interviews. In the process of completing career conversations, students often develop relationships with professionals who become advocates for them during the hiring process. In addition, the experience of having career conversations makes those students more comfortable during interviews than students without this experience. At the end of most formal job interviews, the interviewer gives the candidate an opportunity to ask questions. Candidates experienced with career conversations can look at this opportunity kind of like a mini career conversation. (Asking the person to walk you through their whole career wouldn't be appropriate, but most other common career conversation questions would be.) Most importantly, students with experience in career conversations build their self-confidence in talking with professionals with whom they are meeting for the first time.

> *Always do your best. What you plant now, you will harvest later.*
>
> —OG MANDINO

When it comes to the job search, most resources focus on résumés, cover letters, and interviewing skills. Your college's career center likely has excellent resources available on these topics and I encourage you to utilize them. Here, I want to emphasize some of the most important interviewing techniques and to provide tips on how to mentally prepare for interviews and handle rejection.

The first key to mastering job interviews is to understand that there are many different types. Behavioral interviews are the most common; you describe your strengths, skills, and talents, how you behaved in a particular situation, or dealt with a specific problem. Case-based interviews are just that; they present you with a case and you explain your analysis of the situation and the actions you would recommend or take yourself. There are two main variations on this approach. In one, you discuss the case with other candidates, in front of evaluators (who are paying attention not only to your knowledge but also to how you interact with others in a problem-solving situation). In another, you take the case (or problem statement) home and return to make a presentation to the hiring team, offering your analysis and responding to their questions. For more technical positions, you could be subjected to tests for hard skills (such as solving a mathematical equation, correcting software code, identifying cells, or something similar).

These are the most common types of interviews. In this chapter, I am focusing on how to succeed in behavioral interviews.

There also are many interview formats, including in-person, video, phone, automated (in which you use your computer to record your answers to questions), and group interviews. If you are unfamiliar with an interview type or format, it's always helpful to speak to a career counselor, friend, or mentor who has experience with a particular interview format. Your school's career center also may have valuable platforms available to you for practicing interviews.

> *Good stories . . . make us think and feel. They stick in our minds and help us remember ideas and concepts.*
>
> —SHANE SNOW

KEY TAKEAWAY #1: THE IMPORTANCE OF USING STORIES

Students who are most successful in receiving job offers have told me that stories are the path to mastering job interviews. For entry-level positions, there often is a slim margin between students who get hired and those who don't. Your ability to tell stories that showcase why you will excel in the role for which you are applying is fully within your control and can be strengthened through practice, regardless of your experience or life circumstances.

Many students don't thoroughly prepare for behavioral interview questions because these questions seem so easy. For example, let's consider the common question, "Tell me about yourself," asked at the beginning of most interviews. This question is an opportunity for you to give a two-minute summary of who you are, why you believe you are a good fit for the position, and what strengths you would bring to the role. But many students answer quickly, in twenty seconds, and just say their major or recite descriptive information from their résumé. Other students ramble aimlessly for five minutes. What a missed opportunity! When preparing your answer to "Tell me about yourself," consider how you might paint a clear picture of why you will excel in the role *as if those two minutes were the only chance you had to earn the internship or job.*

Example "Tell Me About Yourself" Answers

Here are three examples showing different effective ways to answer "Tell me about yourself." As you read them, notice both the content and the structure of the answers, and reflect on whether that model could work well for your own answer. The first is for a student interviewing for a graphic design summer internship.

> I was born in Arkansas and I have a big family, with two sisters and two brothers. Growing up, I spent a lot of time in the forest near my house, and I've always been fascinated by the natural patterns in forests. I would often bring home leaves and tree bark and make art out of them. As I got older, I realized that I had a passion for design, especially design inspired by the natural world. I love how graphic design can be used to share a message or an emotion without even using words.
>
> Last summer, I did some volunteer work for an environmental nonprofit in my town, helping them design marketing materials and social media graphics. My designs ended up helping the organization double its social media followers and run a successful summer launch event.
>
> I'm really excited about this internship opportunity because I believe that I can use my design and communication skills to add value to your organization.

You'll notice the elements of this strong answer: very brief background on the student's background, a unique personal story, evidence of the student's skills, and a conclusion that showed why the student wanted the internship.

Here's a different way to answer the question that is equally effective, this one for a teaching position.

> I'm really passionate about teaching because I've had amazing teachers who have been influential in my life, and I want to be a role model and mentor to other students. For the past three years, I've studied psychology at University of Idaho, and I've had several experiences that helped me decide to pursue teaching and that taught me valuable skills in conflict management and creativity.
>
> Two years ago, I worked as a teacher's assistant at a small private preschool. The kids I worked with had special needs, so they struggled to sit still or listen to the teacher. One of the boys also frequently hit other children. Over the course of two months, I devoted lots of attention to caring for the kids I worked with, mediating conflicts and setting them up for success. At the end of my time at the preschool, the parent of the boy told me that they were really grateful for my support and that they wanted to hire me to babysit their son.
>
> Second, during the past school year, I worked with junior high students in an after-school program. As you can imagine, it was quite different from working with preschoolers! Many of the kids spent most of the afternoon on their phone. I decided that I would create an activity so exciting that they would want to join. By getting to know some of the students and their interests, I created a sort of "mini Olympics" that lasted for two weeks. Not only did the students get off

their phones and fully participate, but also new students joined the program because it looked like so much fun.

These two experiences working with the preschool and the junior high showed me that I enjoyed working with kids of all ages, and I learned some valuable lessons along the way. I'm interested in this teaching role to further my skills as an effective educator and to make a positive difference in the kids' lives.

Rather than telling one cohesive story dating back many years, this student chose to focus on two concrete experiences she had during college and what she learned from them. She started her answer with why she was passionate about teaching, then used concise language to show that she was collaborative, smart, empathetic, creative, and good at problem solving. The interviewer would likely remember her stories and the two skills she emphasized: conflict management and creativity.

Here's one final example, for a medical assistant position, from a student who attended a junior college and didn't have traditional job experience because of his family circumstances.

My number one value is helping others. I was raised by a single mother, and all throughout junior high and high school, I was working odd jobs to help provide for my family. I started by mowing lawns for neighbors, then worked at a restaurant, and finally worked unloading delivery trucks at a grocery store. After high school, I decided to attend junior college because it would allow me to live at home and help out my family. All through my first two years of college, I was working late nights at the grocery store, then had to wake up early for classes. The schedule was really tough, but I stayed focused on what was best for my family.

Last year, my younger brother broke his collarbone, which was really difficult for our family because of the medical bills and trips to the doctor's office. On several occasions, I spent time with him at his appointments, and every time, I was impressed by the kindness of the medical assistants working there. I decided that working as a medical assistant would be a great way to serve others, and that's why I'm interested in this job. I know I don't have any formal medical experience, but I'm confident that I will put in the effort to succeed in this role and provide empathy and kindness to everyone I work with.

This student did an excellent job of using his personal story to show that he was hardworking and cared deeply about his family and helping others. He had a memorable opening sentence and did a great job of telling his story in a way that was humble but also clearly showcased his competencies. Many students mistakenly believe that interviewers only care about professional experience. This isn't true. Depending on your background, personal stories like the one this student shared can be an incredibly effective way to demonstrate the value you can provide to an organization.

You should be creative and choose the approach that you think will be most effective for telling your story and responding to "Tell me about yourself." It is important to be clear about why you want the role, to provide some information about your background or interests that helps humanize you, and to use a story, or stories, to demonstrate some of your skills.

Your Answers Need Proof

Recruiters and hiring managers will ask themselves questions such as *Would we like to work with this individual? How well will she fit into our team or culture? Does he have the necessary initiative and work ethic to meet our demanding schedules?*

Let's take a look at the difference between a weak and a strong answer to the behavioral question "What are your greatest strengths?"

A *below-average answer* is purely descriptive. For example, you might say, "I'm hardworking, I'm detail oriented, and I'm a team player." These statements might all be true, but if this is all you say, the interviewer has no reason to believe you. You must provide evidence in the form of short, engaging anecdotes about your experience that demonstrate how hard you work, your attention to detail, and an ability to get along with colleagues.

An *above-average answer* could provide the same characteristics but would support each with a short story, or use one story that encompasses multiple strengths. Your story should include context on the situation, a challenge or problem that needed solving, the actions that you took (not that the team took; this is about you), and the result of the situation (evidence in the form of numbers is great, if possible). Remember that interviewers are especially interested in your thinking process and how you solve problems. Include specific details so that the interviewer can imagine the scenario and your actions as clearly as possible.

For an answer to this "greatest strengths" question, you might tell one or two short anecdotes that demonstrate your strengths. What's important is that you begin your answer with the characteristics, then provide evidence in story form, then conclude with a rephrasing of your main answer. Here's an example:

> I would say that my two greatest strengths are that I'm dependable under stress and that I'm a team player. Regarding being dependable, my family

runs a small sandwich shop, so I was tasked with helping from a young age. During high school, I would sometimes be the only person working in the shop, so I had to take care of everything: taking customer orders, receiving phone calls, making sandwiches, stocking items, and making sure everything was clean. Sometimes I would need to do three things at once, but I learned to prioritize and do everything I could to make customers happy. I sacrificed opportunities that other students had so my family could count on me.

My second strength is that I'm a team player. During a school project in an English class my first year of college, our team needed to write one research paper, but each team member had very different ideas about how to write their section. I took the initiative to start group discussions about how we wanted to organize our paper and make it cohesive. I also checked in with each team member to support them with their parts of the project. Our professor ended up using our paper as an example of an excellent project in class. So these are two examples of what I consider to be two of my strengths: being dependable and being a team player.

Remember, your answers to behavioral questions should contain proof, through either anecdotes or examples.

Write Down Your Stories Ahead of Time

The best way to ace any behavioral interview is to prepare by first taking notes about—not just thinking about—six to eight stories, or more, of times in your life when you were at your personal best,

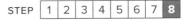

when you took some action that made you proud or that brought a smile to your face. Don't worry about matching a particular story with a specific question. You want to be flexible. During your interviews, if you have already rehearsed these stories (without memorizing them word for word), you will be able to use them to answer a wide range of questions. I call this "pulling a story off the shelf."

Every interview is different, and the questions will vary. You need to be able to adapt. The good news is that most stories can be used in response to various questions. Your stories should particularly demonstrate competencies such as perseverance, leadership, enthusiasm, collaboration, accountability, creativity, and a willingness to learn.

Also, don't write out your stories in sentences. Use bullet points or shorthand notes. Then spend time practicing telling your stories out loud. If you memorize something word for word, you'll sound robotic. Make sure to practice enough that you can *concisely* hit all key points of your stories and relate them to the various questions that are asked.

Here are some topics to help you brainstorm stories:

- A time you showed leadership or persuaded someone to act who wasn't so inclined

- A time you made a mistake, and what you learned from that experience

- A time you had to quickly adapt or learn something new

- An academic or professional accomplishment you are proud of (and why)

- How you went about tackling and solving a difficult problem

- A time you disagreed with a boss or colleague and how you made that situation work out for everyone (be sure, however, never to speak badly about a former boss or colleague)

Two Questions You Must Answer
Even If They Don't Get Asked

Although you will be asked a variety of questions during a job interview, there are two key questions you must answer, regardless of whether they are explicitly asked.

1. **Why do you want the position?** This is somewhat of a trick question. Too often students answer this question selfishly, talking only about how the job will benefit *them*. They might say, "Your organization has a great training program," or "This job will be a great stepping-stone to achieving my long-term career goals," or "Your office is close to where I live," or "I like that I can work remotely." Although these answers are acceptable as secondary reasons, they are not effective ways to begin your answer.

   What you should do is state why you want the role in the context of how you will benefit the organization—that is, how you will provide value to the client, customer, department, and so forth. You might say something like, "I want this job because I'm confident that I can excel at it, and because I will be able to apply my creativity and adaptability to contribute to the design team. In my last role, I did _____ which contributed _____ to the new marketing campaign." Then you might end your answer by saying, "I also know your organization has a great training program, which will help me grow and succeed in the role."

   Hiring managers want to know how you will provide value to make their lives easier and their organization better. They are trying to figure out which candidate is going to provide the best return on their investment (the employee's compensation and benefits).

> *You can have everything in life you want if you help others get what they want.*
>
> —ZIG ZIGLAR

2. **Why are you the best person for the position?** If you're like me, your first thought was "I'm probably not." But that doesn't mean you can't provide a good answer. The organization is likely interviewing dozens of candidates for the position. What is special about you? This is why you need to focus on your individual actions in your stories. Some students have told me they are hesitant to talk about their individual strengths, skills, and accomplishments because they want to be seen as humble. Although you do want to demonstrate your collaboration skills and give credit to other people when that credit is due, your stories should highlight how *your role* in a situation contributed to a larger positive outcome. Perhaps you don't have many accomplishments to point toward. In that case, speak about examples of your best attributes, characteristics, and virtues.

You also should try to develop self-awareness about the unique skills and experiences that you would bring to a role. For example, perhaps you are an engineer with a knack for creative writing. Your writing skills will differentiate you more than your coding skill. As another example, I once had a student studying information technology who was applying for an internship. While the student was qualified, the hiring manager was most intrigued by the student's passion for digital photography that could help with an upcoming project. Maybe you speak a second language that would help you connect with a segment of the organization's customers or partners. Perhaps you have experience in conflict resolution from your childhood circumstances or team projects. Bringing nontraditional skills and showing why those skills can add value is a great way to separate yourself from the competition.

How to Ask About the Decision-Making Timeline

Many students are unsure if it's okay to ask the interviewer about when they will hear about a decision or next steps. Yes, it's okay to ask. You can, and should, inquire. You should leave an interview with a mutually agreed-upon next step. Students have told me the most comfortable and easiest way to ask is to say, "Where do things typically go from here?"

Effective Job Interview Follow-Up

Follow the same best practices you learned in step 7 for career conversations. Send a thank-you email first thing the following morning, and shortly thereafter mail a handwritten thank-you card, if possible. If the interview process drags on, you may also think of ways to say "I'm thinking of you," but with a sentence about your confidence in your ability to do a great job in the position, if hired. You should thank all of your interviewers and anyone who may have organized the interview, such as a recruiter. In most situations, you do not want to send a group thank-you email to multiple people. Take the time to write personalized notes to each person.

Keep in mind that your follow-up often is just as important as the interviews, again helping you to stand out from the crowd. These actions highlight your enthusiasm for the position.

> *It doesn't matter how many times you get knocked down. All that matters is you get up one more time than you were knocked down.*
>
> —ROY T. BENNETT

KEY TAKEAWAY #2: DON'T BEAT
YOURSELF UP IF YOU DON'T GET THE JOB

In one of my classes, a guest speaker named Matthew shared a story about how he let his dream job opportunity slip by. Several months before graduation, Matthew was interviewing for a role with the organization that produces the South by Southwest music festival. His phone interview went well, and he was scheduled for an in-person interview with two hiring managers, one hour with each.

But on the big day, his first interview went so poorly that he was asked to leave before the second interview. He had made a huge blunder.

The interviewer had asked Matthew, "What was your favorite part of your last internship?" Matthew was already nervous, and he had answered the first thing that came to mind. He said, "Well, every Friday the whole team would drink beer together after work."

Obviously, that was an extremely poor answer. The interview wrapped up quickly, and Matthew knew he had screwed up. He was mad at himself for getting so close and then botching the interview.

Yes, Matthew blew it. But there are a couple of lessons to be drawn from his experience. The first is that mistakes are more likely if you aren't adequately prepared. Second, you're not always going to achieve a favorable outcome. This is a contrast to all the other student stories I've shared with you, but I tell you this one so that you won't make a mistake like this. I want you to learn vicariously through Matthew's experience.

I like to remind my students that even though you sometimes don't succeed, it doesn't mean you are doomed for disappointment and failure or that you are unworthy of finding an internship you really want or landing your most aspirational job.

Earlier, I shared one of my favorite quotations, by psychologist Henry C. Link: **"While one person hesitates because**

they feel inferior, another is busy making mistakes and becoming superior." This quote provides a perspective for looking at our mistakes in a positive light. Many times, the only way to improve one's judgement and decisions is through experience, and the price of experience can be temporary failure or making mistakes and learning from them. Don't bounce backward, bounce forward as a result of learning from the experience and doing better the next time around. A major motivation for writing this book is to help you embrace the courageous mindset of Link's quotation.

Sometimes you make a mistake that costs you an opportunity, and other times you will do everything right and not get the internship or job you thought you deserved. You don't have control over other people, and lots of decisions are out of your hands. Sometimes, rejection has nothing to do with you and you don't get to know the reasoning. This is frustrating, I know. I have been there. How you respond is what matters. Allow these experiences to be the impetus that propels you forward with renewed determination and energy instead of getting you down or convincing you to give up.

My students have repeatedly told me that their most important career lessons have revolved around their perspective on failure. By treating mistakes as opportunities for growth and being persistent in the face of failure, you will land an internship or a job that you want.

REVIEW AND REFLECT

- Stories are the route to acing job interviews. Review the list of topics from this chapter and start brainstorming personal examples from your experiences. Remember to include details about the situation, the challenge or task you faced, your actions, and the outcome of the situation for each story.

- Many interviews begin with some version of the question "Tell me about yourself." You should have a two-minute answer prepared that shares a relevant part of your story and describes a skill or experience that can help you succeed in the role.

- During interviews, keep a focus on why you believe you'll succeed in the role for which you are applying and how the organization will benefit from choosing you.

- Reflect on how you typically handle adversity and failure. Setbacks are merely opportunities for growth through learning from experience.

ACTION ITEMS

1. Write down six, eight, or more personal stories in bullet point form. Choose stories that show your leadership, problem solving, growth, collaboration, and how you handle challenges and overcome adversity. Practice saying these stories concisely, out loud.

2. Jot down your answer to "Tell me about yourself" in bullet points. Consider what you can convey that paints a clear picture of why you will excel in the role if those two minutes were the only chance you had to earn the internship or job. Practice out loud.

3. Write down your answers to the questions "Why do you want this job?" and "Why are you the best person for the job?" Even if you are not directly asked these questions, the main points of your answers should come across through your responses to other questions. Practice out loud.

Implementing the Career Launch Method

Inaction breeds doubt and fear. Action breeds confidence and courage. If you want to conquer fear, do not sit home and think about it. Go out and get busy.

—DALE CARNEGIE

The eight steps of the Career Launch Method are meant to be completed more than once. You should be conducting your outreach in manageable stages (reaching out to five professionals every two weeks, for example) and repeating the process with new professionals either when you are not getting responses after following up or when you successfully complete career conversations.

At some point, you will work through your list of twenty-five strategic contacts. If your chosen top ten organizations are small or medium-size, it may be difficult to find more than five professionals from those organizations in your areas of interest. If this is the case, make a new list of ten additional organizations where you would want to work, and repeat all the remaining steps of the Career Launch Method. If some of your initial ten organizations are large corporations or institutions, you likely will be able to contact more than five employees and thus you can repeat the remaining steps with different employees from the same organizations.

I'd like to remind you of a few more resources that can be useful in your career launch journey. Visit **go.careerlaunch.academy**, or go to the back of the book to gain access to the Career Launch Readiness Assessment, a tool that will give you customized recommendations on your strengths, areas for improvement, and actions to take related to your career readiness. I've also included a library of motivational quote backgrounds for your phone or computer, visit **www.launchyourcareerbook.com/quotes**. And, as mentioned earlier, my team and I have created the *Launch Your Career Workbook* with journal prompts, outreach templates, tables to track your outreach and continued follow-up after career conversations, and summaries of key concepts from this book. You can visit **www.launchyourcareerbook.com** to learn more.

Finally, thank you for investing your time to learn about the Career Launch Method. I am rooting for you, and I hope to learn about your wins. Maybe there will be a second edition to this book, and your story will be shared with future students. I invite you to follow Career Launch on LinkedIn at **www.linkedin.com/company/career-launch-programs**, join the Launch Your Career LinkedIn group at **www.linkedin**

.com/groups/13946744, and follow me at **www.linkedin .com/in/seanokeefe**.

If the Career Launch strategies help you succeed, I hope you will pay it forward. You can inspire others to join the Career Launch movement by sharing your success and giving Career Launch a shout-out on social media. Or, you can purchase a copy of *Launch Your Career* for a sibling, friend, cousin, classmate, or someone else important in your life. Or perhaps you'll suggest that your college or an alumni donor buys a copy for every student (we add your school's logo to it and customize a letter on page 1). Lets create a cycle of reciprocity by paying it forward to others.

◆ ◆ ◆ ◆

Your Career Will Be a Journey

It's not what you know that makes the difference. It's what you do with what you know that makes the difference.

—DR. JULIE WHITE

After reading or listening to this book, you now understand the importance of a holistic job search that includes proactively creating relationships with professionals and how following the steps of the Career Launch Method provides access to the hidden job market. You learned about how you can build connections through career conversations, regardless of the size of your existing network. And you learned that through effective follow-up and asking the right questions, you can turn your career conversations into formal job interviews.

This path requires persistence and determination, but I know you have the inner strength to take these steps and to build confidence along the journey. You know what it takes and you know what to do. It's time to turn that knowledge into action, if you haven't already started.

Thus far, we have focused on how to get a job. And I sincerely hope that you land a job you want. But I also know from experience that students often get a job on their top ten list, only to find it unfulfilling or different than they expected. Others realize that their dream job forces them to make large sacrifices in other areas of life, or that a job clashes with their values—or that their priorities have changed. Maybe the job you really want requires long hours, or a low salary, or moving to a new city. These tradeoffs are part of life, and you'll decide what's best for you.

Most of my students are between the ages of eighteen and twenty-five, a period in life that features numerous twists and turns as students discover their values and discern their vocation. At this age, you simply may not have enough experience to have clarity. That's okay. Only a small percentage of students know their career goals from the time they are teenagers and stick with the same goals throughout their career.

I want you to know that *it's completely okay if your your priorities or interests change*. Finding a meaningful career is an iterative process; through experimentation, you can find new ways to grow and express your skills. And your ideal career should mesh with your other values, such as family, friends, health, hobbies, spirituality, lifestyle, personal growth, flexibility, and service to others.

In chapter 1, I shared my story of landing internships with companies on my top ten list and then a full-time job with the

Oakland A's—a dream job at the time. But what happened next in my story illustrates how one's vocation and priorities can evolve.

> *The inner speech, your thoughts, can cause you to be rich or poor, loved or unloved, happy or unhappy, attractive or unattractive, powerful or weak.*
>
> —RALPH CHARELL

OVERCOMING IMPOSTER SYNDROME

During my seven years working for the A's, I had the opportunity to make significant contributions and to set several records for business development and corporate partnerships. But I realized the job wasn't my true vocation. In college, I had placed an extremely high value on the brand name of the companies where I interned and desired to work after graduation. As I matured, I became more intrinsically motivated and I wanted more opportunities to lead and serve others.

I began studying for my MBA at Santa Clara University in 2005 and attended a study abroad trip to China and South Korea organized by Barry Posner, who was then the dean of the Leavey School of Business. On the thirteen-hour flight across the Pacific, I had the good luck to sit next to Barry. We started chatting and he asked me about how I had landed my job with the Oakland A's, assuming I had an inside connection.

I was irked by the phrasing of the question, because I didn't have any connections! I told Barry the story of my journey from Professor Ferrer's class to the Oakland A's, and how grateful I was for the guidance I had received. I told Barry that I was thinking of starting an organization to provide workshops and seminars about career empowerment to college students.

Barry encouraged me to do so. Then, later in the plane flight, he asked me, "How would you like to teach a class at Santa Clara University to share your career experiences with students?"

At first, I thought this was a joke. How could a twenty-seven-year-old with average grades as a communication major be qualified to teach in the business school at Santa Clara University?

But I realized he wasn't joking. He said, "We have a business leadership class that is not about how to be a CEO one day; it's about how to be a leader right now—regardless of your age and background. Your message of taking a proactive approach to career goals would fit perfectly into the curriculum. Moreover, the class is primarily taught by adjunct faculty."

It sounded like the opportunity of a lifetime, but my mind was racing with "imposter syndrome," feelings that I didn't share with Barry. Imposter syndrome is defined as a collection of feelings of inadequacy that persist despite evident success.[1] People with these feelings suffer from self-doubt even when they see evidence of their competence. Many people, even highly successful people often suffer from imposter syndrome, but it's not the same as low self-esteem or a lack of self-confidence.

Instead of sharing my fears, I responded with, "That sounds great."

Barry went on to say, "I don't want to get ahead of myself. You'll need to finish your degree, and I can't guarantee you'll get the position, but I will recommend you for an interview."

After earning my MBA, I followed up with Barry and was given an interview with the department advisers. The interviews went well and I taught my first class beginning in January 2010. I had the opportunity to share my career journey, to encourage students to take a similar approach, and to pay forward Al Ferrer's mentorship.

I must admit that I was extremely nervous before my first two class sessions. But during the third class—and I remember this like it was yesterday—as I was engaged in a class discussion about career conversations, a feeling came over my body, a sense that impacting students was what I was meant to do with my life.

I knew I had found my next career. But sometimes pursuing your next career comes with sacrifices.

> *It is the ultimate luxury to combine passion and contri-bution. It's also a very clear path to happiness.*
>
> —SHERYL SANDBERG

THE $200,000 PAY CUT

Around the same time that I taught my first class, I joined an eighteen-person company called Shamrock Office Solutions, where I was the vice president for business development. Even though the industry (printers, photocopiers, and information technology services) was a lot less appealing to me than professional sports, I had much more fulfillment in my seven years with Shamrock than I did with the Oakland A's. I had a lot of responsibility for the growth of the organization at Shamrock, which was something I craved at the time. I had an incredible mentor, Brian Driscoll, and as we grew, I had the opportunity to mentor other leaders, who eventually took my place.

Despite the success and fulfillment, I realized that my ikigai was in teaching and coaching college students. As I continued to teach classes at night for the next six years, I knew that helping students find meaningful careers was my vocation and my new dream job.

In early 2016, I had a choice to make. A position opened to teach business communication as a lecturer at Santa Clara University. My supervisor at Santa Clara encouraged me to apply. But I initially thought that I couldn't pursue this dream job because it didn't pay well enough. My wife, Jaclyn, and I are planners, and we had anticipated that I would continue to work in a higher-paying industry until my fifties so that we could save for a comfortable retirement with lots of travel and for our kids' college. A teaching position would drastically alter our plans, so I didn't even tell Jaclyn it had become available.

But over the next few weeks, the opportunity gnawed at me. I finally spoke with Jaclyn and we decided that I should at least apply.

I ended up being offered the job. After discussing with Jaclyn, who was very supportive, and taking time to reflect, we decided I should take the position. We sacrificed significant income, but we were able to make it work because we had been living below our means. We realized that many people never truly find their vocation, and I was fortunate to have found mine at a relatively young age. We decided to value service to others over money.

In 2018, with encouragement from Erin Kimura-Walsh, Santa Clara University's director of First-Generation Student Programs, and Rose Nakamoto, Santa Clara's director of Career Services, I founded a social enterprise called Career Launch to partner with colleges and career programs to help solve the job/internship search equity problem. According to the Social Enterprise Alliance, a social enterprise is an organization that addresses a basic unmet need or solves a social or environmental problem through a market-driven approach.[2] In 2019, Santa Clara University provided Career Launch with financing to scale its impact nationwide. Also in 2019, I received requests to write this book, mostly from higher education professionals who attended conferences where I spoke. I never thought I'd be an author!

My path has not been linear, and yours might not be, either. I've learned that practicing discernment, being intentional, creating relationships, gaining skills and compentencies, working hard, and following my intuition were all keys to discovering a career that I love. I hope my story provides a helpful perspective that you can reference as you navigate your career.

> *Define success on your own terms, achieve it by your own rules, and build a life you are proud to live.*
>
> —ANNE SWEENEY

THE SEVEN PILLARS OF LIFE AND SETTING GOALS

I began writing down my goals when I was in college, working for the kitchen knife company Cutco, but my goals were always career focused. In my midtwenties, I realized that this method of goal setting was not optimal, because I wasn't thinking holistically about my life. Over a period of a few years, however, I realized that there were seven main pillars of my life that I valued:

1. Family and friends

2. Contribution to society

3. Spirituality

4. Health

5. Career

6. Education/personal development

7. Lifestyle

In my early twenties I had been excelling at career but lagging behind in my contribution to society and my spirituality. Once I realized that all seven pillars were important to my well-being, I began evaluating myself in each area, giving myself letter grades to track my progress, and setting goals more frequently, and with more specifics.

My wife and I now set quarterly goals for each pillar. Our overarching goal is to be giving ourselves As in each category, but inevitably we sometimes need to make sacrifices in some areas to make progress in others during different periods of life.

You don't need to agree with all seven of my pillars, but I encourage you to spend time thinking about the areas of your life that you value and to set quarterly goals. Note: You'll want to write down your goals and put them in a place where you see them frequently. Simply thinking about your goals is not enough. A Dominican University study showed that participants who wrote down their goals were 50% more likely to achieve them.[3]

While career will likely be one of the pillars that are important to you, it probably won't be the only one. You may need to make sacrifices in the years ahead by spending more hours at work in order to be successful in other areas later on. Many students don't have clarity on all their values, much less to be able to map out a life that gives them fulfillment in all the different areas at all times. So give yourself compassion, and always be working toward living more in line with your values.

Regardless of which life pillars you decide on, writing down your goals and regularly evaluating yourself in your chosen areas will help you in your career and beyond.

I believe a meaningful life should not be measured by your possessions, job title, or things like your number of social media followers; it should be measured by personal growth and service to others. Life is not about what you have. It's about what you *do* with what you have.

Your life is a gift to you. How you serve others is your gift to the world.

Thank you for investing your time in this book. I wish you great success in your career and life journey.

RESOURCES

The Career Launch Readiness Assessment

The Career Leadership Collective, along with my Career Launch colleagues and I have created a tool for you to discover your level of professional readiness: the Career Launch Readiness Assessment. The recommendations from the assessment do not replace the Career Launch Method; they complement it by showing you your strengths, areas for growth, and what you can do to improve your professional readiness. Visit **go.careerlaunch .academy** to take your assessment.

The Career Launch Readiness Assessment contains a total of forty statements that address the essential actions and behaviors that students use to land internships and jobs. You can take the assessment up to three times. Ideally, you follow our recommendation at the beginning of the book and take the assessment right away, and then again after completing the book and the action steps within. It takes about ten minutes to complete. Each of your responses will range from 1 (*Strongly disagree*) to 5 (*Strongly agree*). You will be assessed in five areas:

- Career exploration

- Personal branding

- Relationship building

- Career search

- Personal growth

After completing the assessment, you will be given access to receive a PDF report with your scores in each of these five areas, along with customized recommendations about how you can improve your professional readiness in each area. These recommendations include videos to watch, articles to read, reflection questions, actions to take, and more.

Colleges: A co-branded landing page, with access for only students from your school, can be available for bulk purchases. Email **impact@careerlaunch.academy** for more information.

The Five Keys to Entry-Level Compensation Negotiation

If there's anything that students fear more than cold networking, it's salary negotiation (or public speaking). Negotiating your compensation can make a huge difference over the course of your career, and it is well worth the temporary amount of initial discomfort. Even if you don't get what you ask for, negotiating—the right way—is worth it because you demonstrate that you are someone who is comfortable engaging in difficult conversations, which is a sign of a future leader.

Carnegie Mellon University professor Linda Babcock talks about the difference that salary negotiation can make over the course of a long career. She says, "I tell my students that by not negotiating their job at the beginning of their career, they're leaving anywhere between $1 million and $1.5 million on the table in lost earnings over their lifetime." Your future salaries are based in part on your past salaries, so small differences like negotiating a starting salary of $48,000 instead of $45,000 can make a big difference over a long period of time.

Many students fear that negotiating will make them appear to be pushy, demanding, or ungrateful. It is important to be grateful for a job offer or promotion, especially during tough economic times. But let me reiterate: negotiating your salary—the right way—makes you look like a leader who takes initiative and is comfortable having difficult conversations in a professional manner. Even if you aren't successful, you win. The fact that you are willing to engage in an uncomfortable conversation says a lot about you and your professional brand.

Facebook and Google executive Libby Leffler says, "I know when [candidates who negotiate] are in their roles for me, they're going to negotiate whatever it might be. They're going to work with a partner to get something done; they're going to work with the sales team to make something happen; they're going to be able to achieve a compromise with a cross-functional team so that we can move a project forward." In short, negotiation can impress an employer regardless of results.

There are five keys to entry-level salary negotiation. The first two involve what not to do before getting a written offer, and the next three are about what to do once you have a written offer in hand.

1. Don't Be the First Person to Give a Number or Range

If any recruiters or hiring managers ask about your salary requirements during the interview process, you should avoid saying a number or range. Instead, you can respond to salary-related questions during the interview process with the following response:

> At this point in the process, I'm focused on finding the right fit. I'm confident that when I do, salary and compensation will not be an issue.

If you are further pressed to give a number, you can ask:

> What is the standard range for this position?

If they give a number or range, you simply respond by saying:

> Thanks for sharing. That won't be an issue.

If they don't answer your question directly, they will likely say, "The range is based on qualifications and experience." To which you should reply:

> I understand. Of everyone that has been hired for this position in the past two years, what is the lowest and highest salary and compensation someone has received?

Note that this question doesn't work for start-ups or brand-new positions.

Here's the logic behind this rule: If you give a number that's below what the organization was expecting, they will likely think you'll be happy with this amount, and thus you may be offered less than you would have been otherwise. If you give too high a number or range, they might eliminate you from the interview process because they know they won't be able to afford you, and it doesn't make sense for you to continue in the interview process. Therefore, it is best practice to avoid providing a number or range until you receive a formal offer in writing.

2. Never Negotiate Before You Have a Written Offer

As a job candidate, you don't have any leverage or power until you receive a written offer. The employer has all the power, because there likely are many applicants for a limited number of positions. You don't want to take the risk that something you say during negotiation could prevent you from receiving a written offer.

Many employers will strategically provide a verbal offer and ask the candidate to commit verbally on the spot, before providing a written offer. One of the reasons they do this is because once you verbally commit, it's difficult for you to ask for a higher salary or more benefits.

If you have a call or meeting where you receive a verbal offer, you should avoid committing on the spot *even if you are sure you'll accept the job.* It is best practice to ask for the offer in writing. You also shouldn't try to negotiate salary when you receive a verbal offer. Even at this point, you still have very little power or leverage.

You want to say something like:

> Thank you, this sounds great. I'm really excited about joining the team. My [professor/family/mentors] have told me it's best practice to review an offer letter in writing and sleep on it before signing. I imagine that you will be sending the offer in writing soon, is that correct?

In this way, you express your enthusiasm about the position while giving yourself a chance to review the offer and set up a follow-up conversation to inquire about the compensation package.

Once you have the offer *in writing,* move on to number 3.

3. Set Up a Live Meeting with the Hiring Manager

At some organizations, you may get a written offer from a recruiter or someone other than the person who is going to be your supervisor. If this is the case, you want to ask for a meeting with your soon-to-be supervisor, not the recruiter. Even if the offer is emailed to you by the recruiter or human resources professional, you should follow up with the person to whom you'll be reporting.

In your email to your supervisor, say something like:

Hi, [Name],

Thank you for the offer. I'm really excited about joining the team. I have a few questions that I would like to discuss with you.

Would you be able to chat within the next few days?

Regards,
[Your Name]

Just as with a career conversation, you want a video chat or in-person meeting, not a phone call, if possible. Definitely do not try to negotiate over email.

4. Ask "Do you have any flexibility?"

During your meeting, you should not ask your compensation question first. Instead, start by expressing gratitude for the offer and asking genuine questions about the job role, organization, or work environment.

After asking a few of these other questions, you can bring up the topic of compensation. I recommend using the question:

Do you have any flexibility in regards to salary?

In my experience as a job seeker and as a hiring manager, this is the most simple and professional way to engage in salary negotiation. There is no chance that you will have your offer rescinded if you ask the question in this manner.

There are a few common responses you will receive to this question. The first possibility is that the person will say no. If this happens, you can either sign the offer letter as is or ask if they have flexibility on any other aspects of compensation, such as health care, tuition reimbursement, a gym membership, a transportation stipend, a signing bonus, stock options, moving expenses, and the like.

The more likely possibility is that they answer something like, "Possibly. What do you have in mind?" Be prepared for this question. You should do your research before the conversation to know what salary increase you have in mind. This figure should be based on your research from a credible website and supported by saying how you will add value to the role.

As an example, you might say:

> Based on my research of comparable positions and the value I believe I will add to the team, I think a base salary of [$55,000] would be appropriate. Can you make that number work?

This ending question is direct, gets right to the point, and maximizes your chance of getting a favorable response. You don't want to be wishy-washy or long-winded. You also might be asked about the comparable positions, so you need to be able to cite your source(s).

And if you receive a no, you can accept the offer as is, knowing that you just gained some respect and positive brand image in the process. Remember, leaders and future leaders are people who know how to handle difficult conversations professionally.

5. Ask About Years Two and Three

Regardless of the answer you receive to your question about compensation flexibility, there's another question I advise you to ask:

> Assuming I do an outstanding job in this role, what is the opportunity for my compensation to increase at the end of my first year and second year?

The other person's answer to this question will allow you know what to expect for your earning potential. This will give you peace of mind and insight into your short-term earnings opportunity.

Your question also can be the first step in one more negotiation strategy. If you feel like your soon-to-be supervisor wants to help you but can't do anything about increasing the initial job offer, you can then say something like:

> Okay, that is great to know. Thank you for sharing. Can I ask another question?
>
> (*Pause and let them reply*)
>
> Would you be willing provide me with a job review after six months, and if you determine that I'm doing an outstanding job, can I earn the year-two compensation increase after six months?

By asking this question, you are giving yourself a chance (six months) to prove your value to the organization, and they may be willing to increase your salary more quickly. Even if you get a no, you will have a better idea about what kind of increases you can expect if you excel in the role.

Take the story of one of my students, Torben, from 2018. Another student, Marina, had an almost identical story in 2021.

Torben received a verbal job offer from the number one company on his top ten list. Following my advice, he asked for the written offer letter during the verbal offer. Once he received the offer via email, he reviewed it, and then emailed the supervisor and was able to set up a meeting. He started by asking noncompensation questions, and the conversation was going well. Then he asked his soon-to-be supervisor if there was flexibility in the salary. The response was that there was no possibility to increase the starting salary, and Torben was told what he had been told throughout the interview process—that everyone in the same position, in the same geographic area, earned the same amount.

He proceeded to ask about the opportunity for compensation increases at the end of his first year and his second year. He was thrilled to hear the answers.

Torben thanked the manager and signed the offer.

Six days later, he was surprised to receive a new offer letter in his email inbox. The letter was exactly the same as the one he had signed, but the starting salary was $3,000 higher! The supervisor either had the authority to make the increase or had put in a good word for Torben with their supervisor or with human resources. Either way, Torben's effort had paid off—even after hearing an initial no.

Think about all the positives that Torben generated because he was willing to ask about salary and compensation flexibility. Financially, he received an immediate increase in pay and put himself in position to earn more income throughout his career. In terms of mindset, he now had clarity about his short-term earning potential. And from a personal brand viewpoint, he was now more respected and more likely to be seen as a future leader. Not bad for a couple hours of effort.

Torben said, "I was extremely nervous about negotiating with a company I really wanted to work for. I had an offer from my number one company. But as I thought about all the tips I learned, I realize that nothing I planned to say would put my job offer at risk. As long as I followed the suggestions, there was virtually no downside and a lot of upside."

Motivational Quote Library

In my classes, I give my students printouts of inspiring quotations on card stock paper. My students often tell me they hold on to these quotes years later and hang them on their wall for inspiration. I've included some of my favorite quotes throughout this book, and I hope you have found some of them to be motivating and useful.

In the spirit of inspiring you to take action in your career and life, my team and I have created a set of phone and computer screen backgrounds for you to download. Go to **www.launchyourcareerbook.com/quotes** to access your free backgrounds.

Examples:

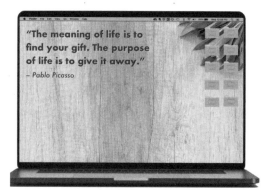

Career Launch Certifications: Career Counselors, Coaches, Student Affairs Professionals, and Faculty

This book, and the *Launch Your Career Workbook*, can provide a common language and methodology to make your interactions with students more effective and impactful. If you'd like a deep dive into the best practices for implementing the Career Launch Method, check out our certification programs.

Career Launch Certified Counselor, Coach, Student Affairs Professional

- A high-impact certification seminar
- A copy of the *Launch Your Career* workbook
- Access to coaches-only online resources
- Access to monthly certified-only group sessions for community and Q&A

Career Launch Certified Faculty

- A high-impact certification seminar
- A copy of the *Launch Your Career* workbook
- Access to faculty slides decks
- Lesson plans
- Assignment prompts
- Access to monthly certified-only group sessions for community and Q&A

To learn more, visit **www.careerlaunch.academy/ certifications** and review the testimonials on the next page. If you have any questions, you can email impact@careerlaunch .academy.

Stephen Torres, Industry Fellow & Faculty,
University of California, Berkeley

> "I am proud to be one of the first Career Launch certified faculty recipients. As an educator, the certification allowed me to go deep into the best practices for in-class delivery and course/ assignment design to maximize student effectiveness and output."

Denise Mora, Career Resource Center Coordinator,
North Orange County Continuing Education

> "As the career resource coordinator for our school, I am so glad to be Career Launch certified. I have witnessed how instrumental Career Launch's programming has been to our students. Many of them have landed jobs in the field of their choice, some have been able to enter a graduate program, and all have had an opportunity to build agency, social capital, career development skills, and explore career options."

Tori Bussey-Neal, M.Ed., Success Coach, UC San Diego

> "Career Launch has destigmatized the concept of intentional, proactive networking and has helped my students feel much more confident in their abilities to conduct a holistic internship and job search."

NOTES

Introduction

1. Rebecca Bosl, "Applying Online? How to Improve Your Odds of Landing the Interview," *Forbes*, October 22, 2019, https://www.forbes.com/sites/forbescoachescouncil/2019/10/22/applying-online-how-to-improve-your-odds-of-landing-the-interview/#4940ae59395e.

2. Federal Reserve Bank of New York, "The Labor Market for Recent College Graduates," https://www.newyorkfed.org/research/college-labor-market/college-labor-market_underemployment_rates.html. Updated October 22, 2020.

3. "A Look at the Shocking Student Loan Debt Statistics for 2020," *Student Loan Hero*, January 15, 2020, https://studentloanhero.com/student-loan-debt-statistics.

4. Bill Burnett and Dave Evans, *Designing Your Life: How to Build a Well-Lived, Joyful Life* (New York: Knopf, 2016), 146.

5. Hilary Strahota and Parita Shah, "White Workers Are More Likely Than Black or Latino Workers to Have a Good Job at Every Level of Educational Attainment, Says New Georgetown University Report," *Georgetown University Center on Education and the Workforce*, 2016, https://gallery.mailchimp.com/17c35e53c623b1a2893b0190c/files/ad5b74f3–13b2–4a77–9eab-42bd5899f712/GUCEW_JPMC_RaceAndGoodJobs_PressRelease_10_17_19.pdf.

Part 1: How to Access the Hidden Job Market

1. Burnett and Evans, *Designing Your Life*, 146.

Chapter 2: Habits and Mindsets for Career Success

1. https://www.linkedin.com/pulse/college-students-need-understand-hiring-managers-story-catherwood/

2. Lilledeshan Bose, "Joining Together to Assist Students with Career Readiness," *Bulldog Blog,* University of Redlands, January 24, 2020, https://www.redlands.edu/bulldog-blog/2020/march-2020/joining-together-to-assist-students-with--career-readiness.

3. "Number of Jobs, Labor Market Experience, and Earnings Growth: Results from a National Longitudinal Survey," U.S. Bureau of Labor Statistics, news release, USDL-19-1520, August 22, 2019, https://www.bls.gov/news.release/pdf/nlsoy.pdf.

Chapter 3: Don't Believe These Common Misconceptions

1. Brad Plumer, "Only 27 Percent of College Grads Have a Job Related to Their Major," *Washington Post*, May 20, 2013, https://www.washingtonpost.com/news/wonk/wp/2013/05/20/only-27-percent-of-college-grads-have-a-job-related-to-their-major.

2. NACE Staff, "Employers Want to See These Attributes on Students' Resumes," National Association of Colleges and Employers, December 12, 2018, https://www.naceweb.org/talent-acquisition/candidate-selection/employers-want-to-see-these-attributes-on-students-resumes.

3. Claire Jaja, "The Science of the Job Search, Part VII: You Only Need 50% of Job 'Requirements,'" TalentWorks, November 27, 2018, https://talent.works/2018/11/27/the-science-of-the-job-search-part-vii-you-only-need-50-of-job-requirements.

Part 2: The Career Launch Method

1. Sean O'Keefe and Barry Posner, "Research: Cold Networking Key to Finding Internships and Jobs," National Association of Colleges and Employers, August 1, 2020, https://www.naceweb.org/job-market/internships/research-cold-networking-key-to-finding-internships-and-jobs.

2. Thank you to Rose Nakamoto, director of Career Services at Santa Clara University, for advising us to include this question in our survey.

Step 1: Discernment—Prioritize the Organizations You Want to Work For

1. https://www.naics.com/business-lists/counts-by-company-size/

Step 2: Strategic Research—Discover Professionals Who Can Be Helpful to You

1. Ladders, Inc., "Ladders Updates Popular Recruiter Eye-Tracking Study with New Key Insights on How Job Seekers Can Improve Their Resumes," *PR Newswire*, November 6, 2018, https://www.prnewswire.com/news-releases/ladders-updates-popular-recruiter-eye-tracking-study-with-new-key-insights-on-how-job-seekers-can-improve-their-resumes-300744217.html.

Step 3: Personal Brand—Enhance Your Online Reputation

1. LinkedIn, "About Us: Statistics," https://news.linkedin.com/about-us#Statistics.

Step 6: Advanced Preparation—Turning Career Conversations into Interviews, Recommendations, and Referrals

1. Meta Brown, Elizabeth Setren, and Giorgio Topa, *Do Informal Referrals Lead to Better Matches? Evidence from a Firm's Employee Referral System*, IZA Discussion Paper no. 8175, May 2018, https://ssrn.com/abstract=2441471.

Step 7: Effective Follow-Up—Differentiate Yourself and Build Long-Term Relationships

1. John Wittman, "The Forgetting Curve," https://www.csustan.edu/sites/default/files/groups/Writing%20Program/forgetting_curve.pdf.

Conclusion

1. Gill Corkingdale, "Overcoming Imposter Syndrome," *Harvard Business Review*, May 7, 2008, https://hbr.org/2008/05/overcoming-imposter-syndrome.

2. Social Enterprise Alliance, "What Is Social Enterprise?," https://socialenterprise.us/about/social-enterprise.

3. "The Research: Written Goals Increase Achievement Success," Goalband, http://www.goalband.co.uk/the-research.html.

Special Thanks to Gavin Cosgrave and Barry Posner

Gavin:

What serendipity! Our paths crossed with seemingly perfect timing.

You are not only one of the most talented students I have ever worked with, you are one of the most talented professionals I've ever worked with. Your writing, editing, and design skills are top notch. Your contributions have been vast.

Thank you so much for your partnership.

Barry:

Wow! What a fun journey it has been for me to go from your student to your colleague to a partner on this book.

Your guidance and mentorship throughout the process were critical to bringing this book to fruition. Not only would this book not exist without you, my teaching career and the Career Launch social enterprise would not be a reality if it weren't for your recommending me as an adjunct professor many years ago.

Thank you for being a difference maker in my life.

ACKNOWLEDGMENTS

To my wife, Jaclyn, for your unwavering support in my career journey. I love you. From third grade to infinity :)

Thank you to my son and daughter. I hope you utilize this book when you're in college. I love you. :)

Thank you to my mom and dad for being such great role models. Kelly and I won the parent lottery. I love you. Dad—thank you for our Wednesday meetings.

Kelly, thank you for helping me kick-start the journey of social entrepreneurship from the very beginning. I love you.

To all my aunts, uncles, cousins, family-in-law, and family friends who have supported me and offered encouragement throughout my life—thank you and I love you.

To BG, Siz, Jonny, Lena, Tisa, Costa, Albanese, Phinney, Lutz, Treezy, Dustin, Erik, and Bussa Buss—thank you for your lifelong friendship. Iron sharpens iron. Love you guys.

To Coach Al Ferrer and Stephen Torres. I wouldn't have earned the competitive internships in college without your advice and teachings. And this book wouldn't exist. Thank you for your guidance and for believing in me before I believed in myself.

Thank you to Bill Burnett for writing *Designing Your Life* and for encouraging me to write *Launch Your Career*. Your support was the final push I needed to invest time into this endeavor.

Thank you to The Career Leadership Collective. Two of the best compliments I've received were: 1) Jeremy and Vanessa saying the Career Launch Method sits at the center of the National Alumni Career Mobility survey results about the four highest impact indicators of significant career mobility for students (designing a career plan, receiving helpful career advice, interacting with employers, and seeking career-relevant internships), and 2) being asked to be your partner to scale equitable student success.

Thank you to Steve Piersanti and the BK team. I'm so glad to be an author-member of your social enterprise. It's been a fun process to bring this book to the world. Thank you to those who reviewed and edited the manuscript: Joe Testani, La'Tonya Rease Miles, Vince Menon, Yuli Mendoza, Thomas Vickers, Guisselle Nuñez, Adam Peck, Erin Kimura-Walsh, Stephen Torres, Jenny Williams, Chloe Lizotte, Bruce Goodman, and Chloe Park. Your contributions have made a more cohesive and impactful book. Thank you for your time and feedback.

Thank you to my Career Launch family: Marieli Rubio, Lydia Ku, Alex Pennington, Gavin Gosgrave, Kelly O'Keefe, Ethan Nguyen, Naila Masom, Stephan Vernaelde, Shirley Chan, Liyah Lopez, Joce Pulido, Rapha Guzman, Tim Nile, Adan Gonzalez, Rodrigo Mendez, Celeste Muñoz, Grant Mendoza, Julio Aragon Jr., Ross Urbina, Amita Kumar, JP Rindfleisch, Erin Fox, Yevin Lee, Ashley Landers, Masooda Habib, Christian Ruiz, Jess Recchi, Ryan Klaus, Sarina Jwo, Andrew Papenfus, Camron Tarassoly, Ryan Ohanesian, and Se Kim.

Thank you to Raine Hambly, Gustavo Chamorro, North Orange Continuing Education, and the North Orange County Community College District for being early partners of Career Launch and users of the microlearning programming, the *Launch Your Career Workbook*, and the Certified Career Launch coaching program.

Thank you to those who have played a key role in my career journey: Harry Selkow, Tim Sbranti, Mike Del Ponte, Randy Zechman, Ian Fitzpatrick, Dan Carpenter, Zach Walter, Dominic Dutra, George Anders, Dan Casetta, and David Peralta.

To Coach Kris Lillimagi and Coach Tubbs. You were the first people, besides my family, to believe in me as an undersized offensive lineman. Thank you for the boost of confidence.

To Lisa Wood, Grant Christensen, and David Alioto. Thank you for taking a chance on me as an intern and as a full-time employee. To Brian DiTucci and Adam Clar, thank you for being amazing coworkers and friends. It was a privilege to start the same job on the same day. Rest in peace, Adam.

To Kirk Berridge. Thank you for taking me under your wing and teaching me about the business of sports.

To all the friends I made in business school, especially Dustin Warford, Josh Seidenfeld, Jay Allardyce, Shirley Chan, Seth Tator, Denese Puccinelli, Russ Hearl, Jose Salas-Vernis, and Eileen Long—thank you for being part of my journey.

To my Shamrock family, especially Brian Driscoll, Jason Badger, Zarek Woodfork, Kyle Fraley, Austin Day, Lauren Groth, Phil Benson, John Combs, Dylan Long, and Ryan Bialaszewski— thank you for an amazing seven years.

To my Santa Clara University family. Thank you to Jo-Anne Shibles, Bill Mains, and Brenda Versteeg for approving my appointment as an adjunct faculty in 2010. Thank you to Kirthi Kalyanam and Bill Sundstrom for approving my renewable-term faculty position in 2016, and to Kevin Visconti who encouraged me to apply. Thank you to Desmond Lo for your ongoing support and colleagueship. Thank you to Deirdre Frontczak, Chris Lipp, Toby McChesney, Reggie Duhe, Meghan Cress, and Dennis Lanham, and all my fellow faculty members for your colleague-ship and care for our students. Special thanks to Bill Mains for your friendship and for being in my corner since day one of my

SCU career. Also, special thanks to Erin Kimura-Walsh and the LEAD scholars staff and team of faculty. Erin, you are a remarkable individual. Like so many others, you find a way to give your all to your program and be a great spouse and parent. Thank you for being an early adopter of the Career Launch movement. And thank you for asking me to design and teach a class, for your program is one of the greatest highlights of my teaching career. Thank you, Lydia Ku and Marieli Rubio, for being leaders of the Empowered Students and Career Launch organizations. It brings me great joy to see your growth from being students to being partners/colleagues. Thank you to Rose Nakamoto for all the time you've invested in me and for your contributions to the development of Career Launch. Thank you to Chip Adams for being the reason I finally went "all-in" on helping others scale student impact. Thank you to everyone in the Bronco Venture Accelerator who provided guidance and encouragement to me and Career Launch. Thank you to Father O'Brien for your leadership, and for working with Joe Durepos on *The Ignatian Adventure*. Thank you to Keith Warner, Spencer Arnold, Kristin Kusanovich, Lester Deanes, Caryn Beck-Dudley, Liz Barron-Silva, Eva Blanco, Jen Ferrari, Katy Korsmeyer, Amy Peterson, Melissa Thiriez, Shellie Barber, Priscilla Vallejo, Priscilla Grille, Chris Norris, Morgan Slain, Mike Kovalich, Pam Vavra, Laura Norris, Ruth Davis, Shane Wibeto, Zach Plaza, and Becky Konowicz for your support and encouragement.

Thank you to all my former students, especially Kevin Seng, Isaac Nieblas, Sonya Jain, Veronica Yip, Alex Golden, Anjali Rangaswami, Garibaldi Soedarjo, Henning Jolivet, Janine Bautista, Isabella Draskovic, Ivanna Rivera, Kyle Yi, Max Hedges, Mitch Hansen, Stef Silverio, Torben Billow, Victor Zendejas, Yevin Lee, Brad O'Laughlin, Brenden Haggerty, Erika Harrar, Megan Wong, Roshan Rama, Austin Freitas, Ryan Chien, Matt Silvestri, Trevor Lundquist, Haley Beuligmann,

John Ferrari, Cooper Roach, Gustavo Gutierrez, Stephanie Van, Caleigh Flaherty, Colby Moeller, Classye James, Tiana Nguyen, Juan Rascon-Borgia, Katie VanBenthuysen, Tannaz Azimi, Han Nguyen, Lisa Tanaka, Keith Ho, Claudia Amador, Tamara Zuniga, Martha Herrera Quintero, Robert Armero, Anyce Godoy, Sascha Zepeda, Nicole Figg, Jack Larratt, Jack Tuton, Collin Chan, Alex Kassil, Sabrina Matthews, Lauren Strnad, Caleigh Flaherty, James Kipper, Peter Nestor, Gen Kimura, Bryan Chang, Lauren Kinerk, Jessica Rameriz, Melina Wulin, Samuel Trujillo, Rose Tabares, Marilyn Vasquez, Rocio Cisneros, Hanna Shepps, Kyarra Keele, Wendy Jin, Tou Vang, Madeline Wong, Justin North, Regina Howson, Anne Marie Heywood, Daniel Teramoto, Christine Ha, Jen Nino, Jennifer Chun, Jerry Palacios, Ashley Osornio, Mate Aranyosi, Katie Elkind, Maria Muñoz Yepez, Austin Dickieson, Patty Yuzon, Jorge Estrella, Natali Gonzalez, Jason Chavez, Laura Blevins, Ryan Ebner, Stephen Fraser, Liam Buhl, Esther Landaverde, Amanda Le, Axel Perez, Diego Rojas, Jack Codiga, Kyle de la Fuente, Marialisa Caruso, John Lucier, Nick Wood, Phillip Barber, Aaron Brumbaugh, Colin Yang, Rena Abu-Gharbiyeh, Lyssa Urrutia, Tess Ryan, Yash Garg, Nicholas Platais, Jared Peterson, Rachel Wong, Spencer Stubblefield, Hannah Press, Mahak Kumari, Rachel Wiggins, Axel Hernandez Ruano, Emile Antone, Colman Lin, Daniela Lorenz, James Lungmus, Caleb Zatto, Eoin Lyons, Mary Fowler, Christian Arana, Stephanie Probst, Stephanie Hu, Delia Cuellar, Beau Muster, Aaron Chu, Noah Belkhous, Filip Orth, Sean Meagher, Mark Browne, Justin Gabriel, Karina Sanchez, Ralph Ong, Ashlyn Iwatani, Chris Bui, Michael D'Onofrio, Kosta Bijev, Colby Moeller, Michael DeBoard, Kemper Ray, Andy Meger, Alyssa Lee, and Marc Gehrig.

Thank you to those I've met more recently: Lisa Dominguez, Ron Gonzales, Kat Hait, Tessa Wright, Garfield Byrd, Shawn VanDerziel, Mimi Collins, Lindsay Romasanta, Alison Herr,

Stephanie Estrada, Tori Bussey-Neal, Rachel Rivera, Bev McLean, Brian Dozer, Denise Mora, Ginger Neel, Laurie Eberhard, Mariaelena Marcano, Christy Jewell, Karri Hammertrom, April Farkas, Aliyah Morphis, Ericka Acquaah-Arhin, Lisa McCaffery, Chris Cook, Ray Murillo, Monika Royal-Fischer, Liz Herrera, Lauren Gallagher, Janel Highfill, Maggie Becker, Kelly Harper, Karen McCoy, Lisa Gavigan, Nathan Elton, Margaret Roberts, Robin Nackman, Ryan Atwell, Shayna Carney, Joe Lovejoy, Bill Baldus, Dee Pierce, Ethan Jones, Wil Jones, JJ Smith, Patrick Keebler, Jarret Kealey, Jim Lowe, Nancy Bilmes, Eran Peterson, Katie Puroll, Brian Candido, Brian Barts, Marc Goldman, Jamie Guilford, Betsy Knott, James Tarbox, Jenee Palmer, Merry Olson, Jennifer Baszile, Molly Thompson, Kim Heitzenrater, Eddy Cruz, Ali Rodriguez, Whitley Johnson, Shannon Hargrove, Jay Skipworth, Nina Grant, Cindy Parnell, Angi McKie, Claire Wu, Greg Wurth, Mario Vela, Adrian Rameriz, Amy Shaffer, Leah Turner, Gaston Cantu, Erron Gonzalez, Trish Heard-Welch, Pam Fant-Saez, Cathy Doyle, Everette Brooks, Beth Arman, Johnny Vahalik, Liz Ozuna, Bill Means, Missy Gutkowski, Denise Terry, Jaci Forshtay, Elizabeth Zavala-Acevez, Kelly Dries, Lauren Wooster, and Shenique Rojas-Hyman.

And to those whom I have missed: thank you.

With love and gratefulness,
Sean

INDEX

Note: Figures are indicated by *f.*

About the Author

Sean O'Keefe is a professor, researcher, founder, and speaker. He received the Outstanding Faculty Award at Santa Clara University, which *U.S. News & World Report* ranked among the best in the nation for undergraduate education. Sean also leads a team that conducts research about  college students and the impact of cold and warm networking on building social captial, career readiness, internships, and jobs.

Sean is the founder, partner, and chief impact officer of Career Launch, a social enterprise that partners with colleges and career programs to scale the skill set of launching a holistic job or internship search, especially for students who have few or no connections to the jobs they want.

He is frequently invited to speak at conferences, career expos, professional development summits, and higher education events.

Sean attended Diablo Valley Community College before transferring to earn his bachelor of arts degree in communication at the University of California, Santa Barbara. In college, he created a proactive strategy, now called the Career Launch Method, to land internships with the San Francisco 49ers, Oakland A's, and San Francisco Giants—all without knowing anyone at the organizations. Sean earned his MBA from Santa Clara University and began his teaching career in 2010. He lives in the Bay Area with his wife, whom he met in the third grade, and two children.

You can find Sean on LinkedIn at **www.linkedin.com/in/ seanokeefe**.

About Career Launch

Career Launch is a social enterprise that partners with colleges and career programs to scale the skill set of launching a holistic job or internship search, especially for students who have few or no connections to the jobs they want. Curriculum and programming is  easily integrated into for-credit college courses and into cocurricular programming.

Career Launch provides multimodality programing that includes micro-learning video lessons delivered via text message and email, a corresponding workbook, live video chats offering customized feedback and guidance to students (hosted by Career Launch or by our partner career counselors and success coaches), a "train the trainers" certified Career Launch coaching program, and more.

www.careerlaunch.academy

Dear reader,

Thank you for picking up this book and welcome to the worldwide BK community! You're joining a special group of people who have come together to create positive change in their lives, organizations, and communities.

What's BK all about?

Our mission is to connect people and ideas to create a world that works for all.

Why? Our communities, organizations, and lives get bogged down by old paradigms of self-interest, exclusion, hierarchy, and privilege. But we believe that can change. That's why we seek the leading experts on these challenges—and share their actionable ideas with you.

A welcome gift

To help you get started, we'd like to offer you a **free copy** of one of our bestselling eBooks:

www.bkconnection.com/welcome

When you claim your **free eBook**, you'll also be subscribed to our blog.

Our freshest insights

Access the best new tools and ideas for leaders at all levels on our blog at ideas.bkconnection.com.

Sincerely,

Your friends at Berrett-Koehler

Certified

Corporation

About The Career Leadership Collective

The Career Leadership Collective is a thought-partner and consulting group for colleges and universities that assists executive leaders and career services leaders to systemically weave career  and future preparation into the fabric of the campus experience.

They have done business with more than 850 colleges and universities since 2017 and provide strategic growth consulting and training on topics such as career development–related best practices and diversity, equity, and inclusion analyses. Additionally, the collective hosts conferences, provides online content, and produces the National Alumni Career Mobility Survey, one of the nation's leading alumni career data services.

www.careerleadershipcollective.com